YOUR EXCEL SURVIVAL KIT
A Guide to Surviving and Thriving in an Excel World

by Anne Walsh, MCT

Holy Macro! Books
PO Box 541731
Merritt Island Florida 32954
USA

Your Excel Survival Kit

Author: Anne Walsh, MCT

Copy Editor: Kitty Wilson

Layout: Jill Bee

Cover Illustrtation: Peter Strain

Cover Design: Shannon Mattiza, 6'4 Productions

Indexing: Nellie J. Liwam

Published by: Holy Macro! Books, PO Box 541731 Merritt Island FL 32954

Distributed by: Independent Publishers Group, Chicago, IL

Printed in USA by Hess Print Solutions

ISBN: 978-1-61547-045-7

LCCN: 2016938257

Table of Contents

About the Author

Anne Walsh has been training users in Excel since 1997. She saw her first spreadsheet in the early 1990s and has been curious and intrigued ever since. She has been an MCT (Microsoft Certified Trainer) and MOS Master Instructor since Office 97. She has delivered thousands of hours of training to individuals and businesses, helping users save thousands of hours with the tips, techniques, and shortcuts she shares in class. She likes to bring wit and humour to her classes; one user evaluation said, "I never thought I'd put *Excel* and *fun* in the same sentence." She lives in the west of Ireland, with her very non-techie husband and very techie son.

Dedication

For Bill "MrExcel" Jelen. This is my first Excel book, and I am thrilled and delighted to be the first Irish person on his books.

Acknowledgements

Thanks, of course, to Bill "MrExcel" Jelen, for giving me this opportunity. I also want to thank the "believing mirrors" who have been with me on this journey: Dolores Cummins, Sharon Gaskin (and all the Success Shapers groups I have been part of), Claire Commins, Bróna Clifford, and Karen Gorey.

I also want to thank Kitty Wilson for her work on the book. In the words of my beloved Kate Bush, "It's nearly killing me, but what a lovely feeling" (from "Them Heavy People" on *The Kick Inside*).

Big thanks to Deborah Taylor of www.booklaunchyourbusiness.com. She was the person who advised and helped in the early stages of this book and helped keep me steady when self-doubt was shrieking in my ears.

Also a big thank you to Bróna Clifford, who read the book toward the end and proofread it when I couldn't see it anymore.

I also want to give a mention to my earliest English teachers: Sr. Pius, who lent me books; Mrs. Fennell, who encouraged my imagination and creativity; and Sr. Mary, who taught me accounting and typing—both skills that have been extremely useful to me.

Finally, I offer my deepest thanks to the organisations that have employed me to work with them and for all the great questions I have received from learners over the years.

Introduction

I remember the first time I saw a spreadsheet. It was orange. All of it. (At that time, computer screens showed text in orange or green.) It was a Lotus 1-2-3 sheet, and the various tabs were activated by pressing the / key. I remember feeling both fascinated and tentative as I experimented a bit with it. It was owned by one of the senior managers in the organisation where I was working, so access was rather restricted. That particular spreadsheet added up numbers and did a few other things. Compared to a manual calculator, it was pretty impressive. It was a few more years before I really got to grips with spreadsheets, but the memory of my first stayed with me. (Dare I say the "first row is the deepest"?)

Excel is now the spreadsheet of choice for most users, and that is what this book is about. When I look at Excel, I feel the same way I feel when I am in the presence of great architecture or a beautiful piece of art or music. Yes, of course it has flaws, but I feel inspired by the fierce love and intelligence that have gone into its creation. It is like a great work of art in that every time I return to it, I find something new, I see something new, I learn something new, and I'm not ashamed to say I love it.

I have been teaching Excel for well over 20 years (I've got my 10,000 hours done!), and I still feel joy when I see people's faces light up as they grasp what a pivot table can do for them or when they realise that printing is much easier than they thought. After you have read this book, my hope is that you start to see Excel's power and begin to really leverage it. I feel so privileged when I help people realize that Excel can be their best office friend.

The reality is that in most workplaces—even those with very sophisticated systems—data usually ends up in Excel. If you can get to grips with the concepts in this book, you will soon feel comfortable working with Excel.

Who This Book Is For

This book is for you if you are being asked to use Excel more than you ever expected and you are looking for a guide to take you to what is relevant and most frequently used. It's also for you if you have seen that in your organization, it's the Excel power users who get promoted, and you want to join them.

This book is also for you if you have done any of these things:

- Spent hours or even days trying to produce an analysis that can be done in minutes with a pivot table

- Cleaned up data by clicking on each individual cell (perhaps thousands of times) and pressing Backspace rather than using Trim() to do them all in one go

- Set up repeating data in separate sheets instead of all together in one and then gone through Hell trying to put it all together at the end of the year

- Called on tape, glue, scissors, and a stapler to get an Excel sheet printed on one page instead of on multiple pages

- Manually pulled in matching entries from separate workbooks instead of using the Vlookup() function

- Found yourself in a job where your boss is talking about pivot tables and Vlookup()s, and you have no idea what he/she is talking about—but you know you have to learn fast, and you are terrified

Let me give you a virtual hug if you've been through any of this. And let me reassure you: The madness stops here! It doesn't have to be like this! Excel is on your side. This book is going to get you through. It is, after all, your *Excel Survival Kit*. One of the key things you need to understand about Excel is that it is susceptible to the "garbage in, garbage out" idea, so a good part of this book is about making sure the data you will be using is clean, consistent, and Excel friendly. That's a part of using Excel that I rarely see addressed in Excel books.

What This Book Covers

This book is split into seven chapters:

- **Chapter 1, "Back to Basics: What Do You Know Already?":** This chapter provides a quick intro to the absolute essentials you need to know to grapple with Excel. It shows you how to tackle common tasks like printing, sorting and filtering, and fixing cells. It is set up as a series of numbered steps that you can quickly work through to learn or get reacquainted with Excel basics.

  > **Note** This book comes with files you can practice on. Find these files at www.mrexcel.com/survivalfiles.html.

- **Chapter 2, "Getting Your Data Together: Catching Your File":** This chapter is about getting your data together and, more importantly, assembling your data in a way that makes doing all the other clever stuff with Excel relatively straightforward. This is the secret sauce. This chapter shows you how to set up a list so that your data is entered accurately and completely. It shows you how to set up your data so that you can easily get whatever you need out of it later on. It shows you how to set up a simple list and how to create a list for your recurring data. It's the piece that's often omitted in many Excel books. You get it here.

- **Chapter 3, "Further Cleaning, Slicing, and Dicing":** Yes, at this point you've already got your data into good shape, but you may still need to do further clean-up. This chapter shows you how to remove/complete blank rows, columns, and cells. You will learn some clever quick techniques to clean, combine, and amend existing data. You will also see examples of using formulas to extract specific pieces of data from a data set. You will learn how to identify and remove duplicates and to use conditional formatting to quickly identify the appropriate entries.

- **Chapter 4, "The Vlookup() Function: An Excel Essential":** One of the key tasks in Excel is pulling in and assembling matching data from different sources. To do this, you need to know Excel's Vlookup() function. This entire chapter focuses on this function, including how to use it and also its pitfalls and idiosyncrasies so that you know how to handle this function with speed and care. You will learn how to use it to compare lists and identify missing data (in minutes rather than hours).

- **Chapter 5, "Creating Pivot Tables":** When you need to summarize and present all the data you have so lovingly gathered, cleaned, and assembled, you need to use a pivot table. You can use a pivot table to summarize thousands of rows of data in minutes. A learner once described it to me beautifully as "shrinking your data," and that's what a pivot table allows you to do. You can quickly and easily view your data by months or by various headings. If your boss wants to get a different view of some data and if you have a pivot table, you can deliver the goods in minutes. Moving from manual data organization using filters and sorting to using pivot tables is like moving from walking to driving.

- **Chapter 6, "Using Power Query to Quickly Clean Up Data":** Before this point in the book, you have done a lot of data clean-up manually. In this chapter you learn how to use Power Query to do that work in minutes and, even more amazingly, how to store the steps you take so that all you have to do when you get next month's data is change the data source. Power Query is a game changer, but it's still not very well known beyond the Excel world, so if you learn to use it, you have the inside track. I have to say that every time I use Power Query to clean up data, I feel like a magician—and I want you to feel like that, too.

- **Chapter 7, "Beyond the Pivot Table: Power Pivot":** If using pivot tables is like driving a car, using Power Pivot is like travelling by jet.

Power Pivot allows you to assemble lots of different data sets together without using Vlookup()s and to generate pivot tables with formulas (measures) that allow you to look at your data in all sorts of new ways. Power Pivot is the future of pivot tables, and you'll get a taste of it here.

Typographical Conventions and Special Elements

The following typographical conventions are used in this book:

- *Italic* indicates new terms when they are defined, special emphasis, non-English words or phrases, and letters or words used as words.
- `Monospace` indicates things you type or formulas.
- When I want you to press two keys simultaneously, I use the + symbol. For example, Ctrl+X means you should press the Ctrl and X keys simultaneously.
- When I want you to select multiple items onscreen, I use the | symbol. For example, if I say select File | New, I mean you should select the File tab of the ribbon and then select the New menu item on that tab.

In addition to these typographical conventions, there are several special elements. For example, each chapter includes numbered lists of steps. These lists walk you through processes, step by step. In many cases, I've included screenshots with these lists, to help you understand how what you're seeing syncs up with the directions I'm giving you.

In addition, you will see Notes and Survival Tips:

> **Note** Notes provide additional information outside the main thread of the chapter discussion that might be useful for you to know.

> **Survival Tip** Survival Tips provide quick workarounds and time-saving techniques to help you work more efficiently.

Also, to help you get hands-on practice, I have provided a set of worksheets that demonstrate the concepts described in this book. These files include all the worksheets from the book and sample data. To download the files, visit this book's web page, at http://www.mrexcel.com/survivalfiles.html.

Sometimes when you open the book files, you get a yellow note at the top of the screen that warns you about enabling content (see Figure I-1). Click on this button to work on the file.

 Security Warning   Automatic update of links has been disabled | **Enable Content** |

Figure I-1

Check out my website, www.the-excel-expert.com, for lots of free tutorials, tips, and hints for Excel novices and those of you who are more experienced, Excel adepts.

Chapter 1 - Back to Basics: What Do You Know Already?

Before you really get going on any journey, it's a good idea to step back and check what you know already and what tools you already have. This chapter is essentially a refresher chapter. It reminds you about (or reacquaints you with) the basics—the stuff you really need—so you can get your bearings as you head out into the Excel wilderness.

The goal of this chapter is to remind you of what you know already and to fill in any gaps in your basic Excel knowledge. It begins with getting text and numbers into Excel and then moves on to basic functions and some other worksheet basics. If you think you have forgotten any of this material, now is the time to dust it down out of the Excel attic.

This is meant to be a hands-on book, so to play along, open up a blank Excel workbook and get ready to walk through all the step-by-step procedures presented in this chapter.

> **Note** This book shows Excel 2010 in use, but what this chapter covers is true for all versions of Excel (even if you are rocking an Excel 2003 version).

Data Entry Tips and Tricks

Before you read any further, here are some tips that will make your Excel life a lot easier:

- If you plan to do any calculations with a number, *do not* put any text in the cell with it. When you mix text with numbers and then try to do calculations, Excel gives you a #VALUE! message.

- Try to keep your entries separate. For example, if you are entering names and addresses, and you think that in the future you may want to sort the names by surname, put first name in one cell and surname in the cell beside it.

- If you need to enter phone numbers or any other numbers that have leading zeros (e.g., 00353111155555), type in an apostrophe (') before entering the number. This is how you tell Excel to treat it as text so that it keeps the first two zeros. If you don't do this, Excel keeps removing the first two zeros so you get 353111155555. And like a dog playing fetch, you will spend the rest of the day trying to add those two zeros at the beginning.

> **Note** Have I mentioned that I'm Irish? My spelling and some of my examples may be a bit foreign to those of you from the United States and other places. I'm told that U.S. phone num-

bers never start with two zeros but that a zip code could, in fact, start this way. You may also find other situations where you need to preserve leading zeros.

- Place entries side by side and underneath each other. If you don't, you create a lot of extra work for yourself. Why? Later on, if all your entries are together and you need to sort or filter your list, Excel will naturally sort and filter *all* items in the list.

- Before you can format numbers or text, you need to highlight them. The quickest way to do that is to click on the first cell. Then, keeping your left mouse button pressed down, drag the selection down until you have highlighted the cells you want to apply your formatting to.

Creating a Text Series

1. Click in cell B2 and type January. Note that the cursor is flashing at the end of the word.

2. Rest your mouse pointer in the bottom-right corner of the cell, on the fill handle (see Figure 1-1). (I think of it as a soap opera character named Phil Handle.) It should change to a black cross, but if it doesn't do so, hover the mouse pointer over it until it does.

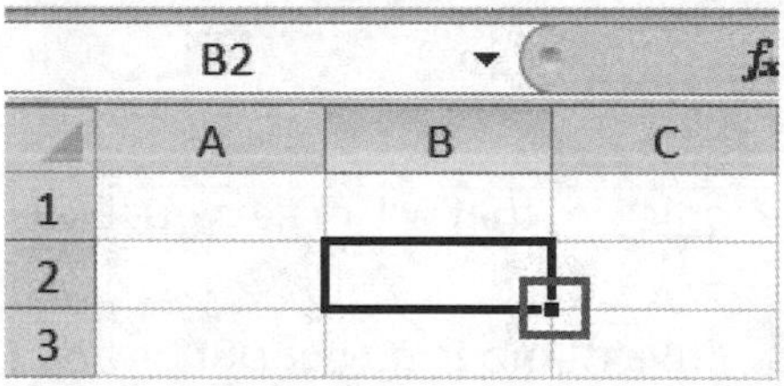

Figure 1-1

3. Holding down the left mouse button, drag the cell down to the cells underneath. You can stop at December, but if you continue, January will reappear.

4. Release the mouse. Holy mackerel! It's a miracle! Excel has filled in the other months. Yep, that's how we do it in the Excel world.

> **Note** You can do the same thing with the days of the week: Type Monday in another cell, grab the fill handle, and drag down. Excel fills in the days of the week for you! Sigh, I love Excel. You can also create your own lists other than the months of the year and days of the week by using the Custom Lists option: Just select File | Options | Advanced | Edit Custom Lists and specify the type of list you want to create.

Creating a Numeric Series

1. Click in cell D2 and type 1.

2. Click in cell D3 and type 2.

3. Highlight both cell D2 and cell D3 by clicking in the centre of D2. Your mouse pointer changes to a white cross.

4. Drag down the mouse until you see a black line around D2 and D3.

5. Rest your mouse pointer on the bottom-right corner of the cell. (Remember Phil Handle?) It should change to a black cross, but if it doesn't do so, hover the mouse pointer over it until it does.

6. Holding down the left mouse button, drag down to cell D11. Holy-moly! Excel does the same neat trick with numbers that it does with words. This time, it fills in the numbers 1–10 for you.

> **Note** Practise with other number sequences, such as 10, 20, etc. and 2, 4, etc. Remember that you have to highlight both numbers, or Excel doesn't know you want a sequence of numbers and just copies the first number, such as 10 or 2, all the way down.

Highlighting More Than One Group of Cells at a Time

1. Highlight the first group of cells you want highlighted (e.g., A2:A4).

2. Press the Ctrl key and keep it pressed down while highlighting the second block of cells (e.g., C2:C4).

3. Release the mouse and the Ctrl key. You now have two ranges highlighted, and when you apply formatting, it applies to both ranges.

> **Note** I refer to *tabs* frequently in this book. By this I mean the set of icons at the top of the screen. For example, File, Home, and Insert are all *tabs* on the Excel *ribbon*.

Formatting Text Entries

1. Highlight the text to which you want to apply formatting.

2. On the Home tab of the ribbon, click on the font formatting you want to apply: B (Bold), I (Italic), U (Underline), etc. (see Figure 1-2). Excel immediately applies the selected formatting to the highlighted text.

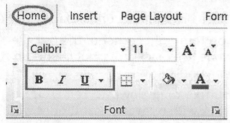

Figure 1-2

> **Note** It is worthwhile at this point to have a look at some of the formatting options on the Home tab. Note that when you rest your mouse on each icon, Excel tells you what that icon does. See, Excel *is* on your side.

Formatting Number Entries

1. Enter some numbers into some cells.

2. Highlight those cells.

3. On the Home tab of the ribbon, click on the numeric formatting you want to apply: Currency, Percent Style, Comma Style, etc. (see Figure 1-3).

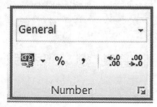

Figure 1-3

Copying and Pasting

> **Note** There are multiple ways to copy and paste: You can use keyboard shortcuts, right-click with the mouse and use the menu that pops up, or use the Home tab of the ribbon. I show only the ribbon method here, but if you prefer one of the other methods, feel free to continue using it.

1. Highlight the data you want to copy and paste.

2. Click Home | Copy.

3. Click where you want the data pasted.

4. Click Home | Paste (see Figure 1-4).

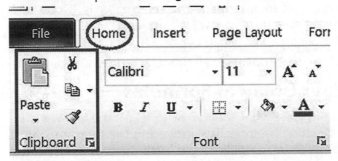

Figure 1-4

Survival Tip If you need to copy the same data somewhere else right away, you can just click in the next location and click Paste again.

Copying Formatting with the Format Painter

1. Highlight the text or numbers that already have the desired formatting.

2. Click Home | Format Painter (see Figure 1-5). A small brush appears on your mouse pointer.

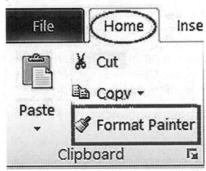

Figure 1-5

3. Highlight the text or numbers you want to apply the formatting to. Excel applies the same formatting to these cells.

Putting the Same Text in Many Cells at the Same Time

1. Click on the first cell you want to add text to.

2. Press the Ctrl key and, keeping it pressed, click on all the cells you want this entry to appear in.

3. Release the Ctrl key. The last cell you clicked is now white.

4. Type the text you want to enter in all the selected cells. (Don't click again, though, or your selection work will be undone.)

5. When you have finished typing the text for all the selected cells, press Ctrl+Enter. Presto! The text appears in all the selected cells.

Dropping Your Dread of Formulas

When I ask people in class what they want to learn, the answer is invariably "formulas," which is rather like answering the question "What books do you like?" with "reading." We'll get further into the nitty-gritty of formulas later in this book, but in this first chapter, we'll keep it pretty basic. The following subsections show the basic steps involved in using the basic operators (+, -, /, *, ()) and some essential functions: Sum(), Max(), Min(), Average(), Count(), and CountA(). You will also see how to fix a cell so that it doesn't move when you copy it and revisit the basics of using worksheets, such as copying, deleting, colouring, etc.

Entering a Formula with the + (Plus) Operator

1. In cell A2, type 100.

2. In cell B2, type 300.

3. In cell C2, which is where you want the answer to appear, type =.

> **Survival Tip** Make sure you have clicked where you want the answer to go. I say this because many times I've seen people with the right answer in the wrong cell because that is where they had placed the cursor when they began the formula. It's sort of "right lover, wrong place".

4. Click on cell A2 and then type +. Even though you click on the number 100, A2 appears in your formula.

5. Click in cell B2 and press Enter. Even though you click on the number 300, B2 appears in your formula. You now see the answer, 400, in cell C2.

The beauty of doing it this way is that if you decide to change one of your entries, Excel updates the values in the formula for you. For example, if you change the entry in A2 from 100 to 500, Excel changes the answer in C2 to 800.

Copying a Formula Down a Column

1. With the formula you just entered still in place in the workbook, in cell A3, type 50.

2. In cell B3, type 100.

3. Click in C2 and drag the Fill Handle down to copy down the formula. In cell C3, you should now see 150.

> **Note** In this case, you have copied down a formula to only 1 row, but the same process applies if you have to copy it down for 100 rows or indeed 100,000 rows. Enter the formula *once* and then copy it down.

Entering a Formula with the – (Minus) Operator

1. In cell F2, type 500.

2. In cell G2, type 100.

3. In cell F3, type 1000.

4. In cell G3, type 250.

5. In cell H2, type = and then click on cell F2.

6. Type a minus sign: –.

7. Click in cell G2 and press Enter. You should now see the value 400 in this cell.

8. Copy down this formula, and you should see the value 750 in cell G3.

Entering a Formula with the / (Division) Operator

1. In cell K2, type 1500.

2. In cell L2, type 100.

3. In cell K3, type 1000.

4. In cell L3, type 250.

5. In cell M2, type =.

6. Click on K2, and then type /.

7. Click in cell L2 and press Enter. You should now see the value 15 in cell M2.

8. Copy down this formula, and you should see the value 4 in cell M3.

*Entering a Formula with the Multiplication Operator **

1. In cell P2, type 500.

2. In cell Q2, type 10.

3. In cell P3, type `1000`.

4. In cell Q3, type `4`.

5. In cell R2, type `=`.

6. Click on cell P2, and then type `*`.

7. Click in cell Q2 and press Enter. You should now see the value 5000 in cell Q2.

8. Copy down this formula, and you should see the value 4000 in cell R3.

Using Brackets in Formulas

You use brackets in formulas when you need Excel to do a particular calculation before it does other calculations. For example, to calculate the total wages eligible for tax, you need to add basic wages plus overtime first—and you can do that by using brackets.

To see how this works, open the file 01_Brackets. In this file you want to add salary and overtime together and then find 20% of this total. In cell E4, the formula $=B4+C4*D4$ has been entered and copied down. You don't have to be an accountant or a tax collector to know that 20% of 8817 plus 215 is not 8860. Of course, if you are a tax collector, you might *prefer* this number.

> **Note** Throughout this book, I many times ask you to open a particular file to play along with the text. You can find these files at http://www.mrexcel.com/survivalfiles.html. Simply download the files and store them someplace you can easily access.

So what has happened here? Excel has found 20% of 214, which is 43, and added it to 8817…and that's how you ended up with 8860.

> **Note** Excel does calculations in a very particular way. Before it does anything else, Excel first looks for brackets and does the calculations within those brackets. Then it uses a particular *operator precedence*: It does multiplication and division before it does addition and subtraction. This is what has happened here. Excel did the multiplication first and then the addition. If you search Excel help for "operator precedence," you will find a more comprehensive explanation of this concept.

But what you want Excel to do is add salary and overtime together *first* and then find 20% of *that*. You do that by using the formula $=(B4+C4)*D4$ and copying it down. (This formula has already been entered into cell F4 in 01_Brackets.) Now you get an accurate answer: 1806.4.

So remember that if you want to force Excel to do a specific calculation first, put brackets around it.

Getting to Know the Common Excel Functions

A *function* is essentially a predesigned formula in Excel. There are functions to handle most of the mathematical operations you might want to do. The following sections cover some of the most commonly used functions in Excel: Sum(), Max(), Min(), Average(), Count(), & CountA().

This is not by any means a comprehensive list of Excel functions. However, these are the ones that you will probably use most often. And part of the beauty of these particular functions is that they all operate in a very similar way.

Adding Up with Sum(): This Is Sum-Thing Good

(Sorry, I Do Love a Good Pun)

1. Open a blank Excel workbook.

2. In cell B2, type 500.

3. In cell B3, type 300.

4. In cell B4, type 250.

5. Click in cell B5 and click Home | AutoSum (see Figure 1-6). You now see the formula =Sum(B2:B4) in B5. You should also now see "marching ants" going around the range B2:B4. This means Excel has included all the cells from B2 to B4, inclusive.

Figure 1-6

> **Note** In Excel, a *range* is any group of cells, and it's indicated with a colon between two cells (e.g., B2:B4 for the range of cells from B2 to B4).

6. Press Enter, and you should now see the number 1050. You've just used your first function!

Copying a Function

All the stuff you have learned already about copying text and numeric data also applies to copying functions.

1. Using the same Excel workbook you just used to try out the Sum() function, in cell C2, type 250.

2. In cell C3, type 300.

3. In cell C4, type 5000.

4. Copy across the Sum() function from cell B5 to cell C5. You should now see the number 5550 in cell C5.

5. Save this file at this point and name it Excel_Practice_1.

Finding the Highest Value with Max()

1. Open the file 01_Functions and in it open the Without Formulas sheet.

2. In cell D6, type =Max. As you start typing, functions appear. After you type M, you get a long list, then after you type MA, the list shortens to the list shown in Figure 1-7.

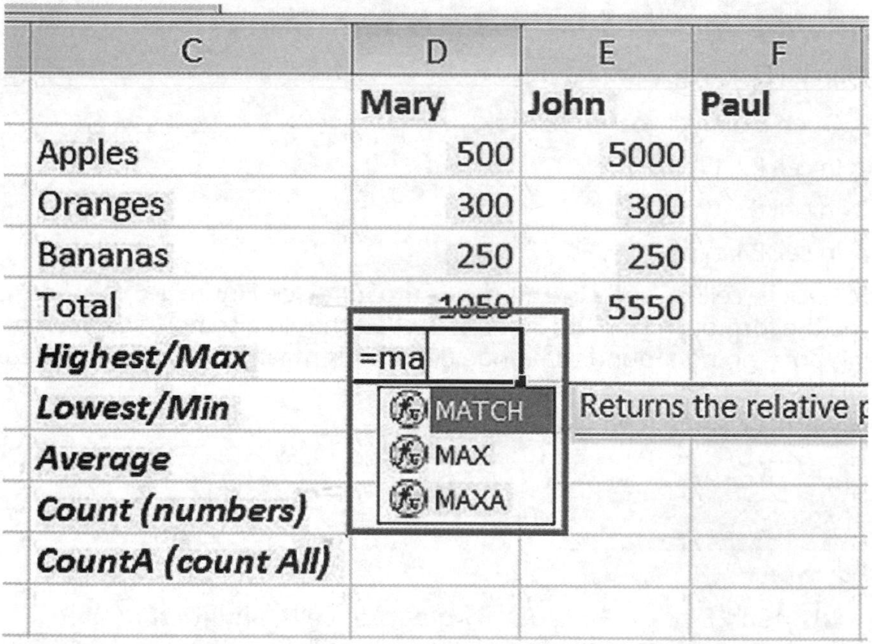

C	D	E	F
	Mary	**John**	**Paul**
Apples	500	5000	
Oranges	300	300	
Bananas	250	250	
Total	1050	5550	
Highest/Max	=ma		
Lowest/Min	MATCH	Returns the relative p	
Average	MAX		
Count (numbers)	MAXA		
CountA (count All)			

Figure 1-7

3. In the list of functions that appears, double-click Max. =Max (now appears in cell D6.

4. Highlight the range D2:D4 (and note that the marching ants appear).

5. Type) and press Enter. You now see the highest value in cell D6: 500. At this point, be careful not to include the total figure in cell D6. If you now copy the formula across to E6, you now see 5000 in that cell.

Finding the Lowest Value in a List with Min()

1. Open the file 01_Functions.

2. In cell D7, type =Min.

3. In the list of functions that appears, double-click Min. =Min (now appears in cell D7.

4. Highlight the range D2:D4 (and note that the marching ants appear).

5. Type) and press Enter. You now see the lowest value in cell D7: 250. If you now copy the formula across to E7, you should see 250 in that cell as well.

Finding the Mean with Average()

1. Open the file 01_Functions.

2. In cell D8, type =Aver.

3. In the list of functions that appears, double-click Average. =Average (now appears in cell D8.

4. Highlight the range D2:D4 (and note that the marching ants appear).

5. Type) and press Enter. You now see the average value of these numbers in cell D8: 350. If you now copy the formula across to E8, you should see 1850 in that cell.

Finding a Count of Numbers with Count()

1. Open the file 01_Functions.

2. In cell D9, type =Coun.

3. In the list of functions that appears, double-click Count. =Count (now appears in cell D8.

4. Highlight the range D2:D4 (and note that the marching ants appear).

5. Type) and press Enter. This function tells you how many numbers you have in the list, and you get the answer 3 in cell D9. When you copy it across to E9, you see 3 in that cell as well because there are three numbers in this list.

Counting Something Other Than Numbers with CountA()

Count() is a very pure, unsullied function in the sense that it will *only* count *numbers*. But what if you want to count how many names you have in a list, such as Mary, John, and Paul? As you see in the Without Formulas sheet in the 01_Functions file, the Count() function does not give you the desired answer. If you try to use Count() in cell G1 with the range D1:F1, Excel gives you 0 as the answer, not 3, because Mary, John, and Paul are not numbers.

In this scenario, you need to use the CountA() function, which you can think of as the "count all" or "count anything" function.

1. In the same file as in the preceding section, 01_Functions, open the Without Formulas worksheet.

2. In cell G1, type =CountA(.

3. Highlight the range D1:F1.

4. Type) and press Enter. Excel says the result is 3. Correct!

Amazing People with Excel Number Magic

One of the things I like to do in class is to highlight some numbers on the screen and then proclaim the average and sum of those numbers. I pause a moment to modestly take in the gasps of admiration, pause briefly to bask in the admiration, and then point out that I, you know, read them from the screen. I reassure them that, in fact, I am *not* Rain Man (from the Tom Cruise and Dustin Hoffman movie about an autistic man who was a mathematical savant). I suppose you would like to amaze friends and strangers like this, too, so I'll share my secret.

Highlight the numbers on the worksheet and then have a look at the status bar (bottom-left side of screen), where Excel provides answers. The status bar gives you at least the sum and possibly also the average of the numbers you have highlighted (see Figure 1-8). Note that if you right-click on this area as well (in the grey area where the numbers appear), you can see up to six answers: Average, Count, Numerical Count, Minimum, Maximum, and Sum.

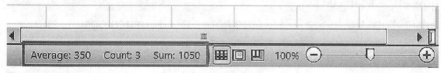

Figure 1-8

If you ever work in an accountant's office, you need this trick because it's an invaluable way of checking to make sure your balances are correct.

Understanding the Copying Functions

So far in this chapter, as you have copied a formula, Excel has automatically adjusted it to reflect the layout of the cells you originally gave to the formula. This is what you want most of the time, and it is called *relative copying* in Excel. The analogy I often give in class is line dancing: When people (or cells) are all lined up to dance and they are told to move to the left, everyone moves to their own left, not to someone else's left (or at least not intentionally…). So it is with the usual copying in Excel: It follows the pattern of adding up cells as given in the first formula and then replicates that.

However, there are times when you want to use one cell (e.g., a tax rate) with a list of numbers. In that case, you need to make one tweak to your formula to ensure that it doesn't change as you copy it down. This is called *absolute copying* in Excel.

The following subsections show these two types of copying in Excel.

Using Relative Copying

1. Open the file 01_Fixing_cells and in it, select the Relative Copying tab.

2. Double-click cell G2. You should see this: =SUM(D2:F2). Essentially, this tells Excel to add up the three cells to the left.

3. Press Enter.

4. Click cell G3. You should see this: =SUM(D3:F3).

The cells listed in the formula in step 4 are different from the ones in the formula in step 2. However, in both cases, Excel is adding up the three cells to the left of the formula. This is relative copying, and it is how Excel usually copies formulas and functions.

Using Absolute Copying to Make Cells Stop Moving

If you want to create a formula that will multiply 10% (in cell H3) by each of the numbers from G4 to G16. If you try your usual copying method first, by clicking cell H4 and entering =G4*H3, you get 10. So far, so good! But now, when you copy it down, it's not so good. If you check cell H7, you see that it says 240000000. A pay increase of 10% on 400 is not, unfortunately, 240,000,000. (You can insert your currency of choice here.) So what has happened?

As you copied down the formula, Excel moved down the cell references as well. So where you see 240000000, Excel has the formula =G7*H6. You need to do something to stop H3 (10%) from changing as you copy it down. Follow the steps below to see what that something is.

1. In the same file as in the preceding section, 01_Fixing_cells, open the Fixing Cells tab.

2. In cell H4, type the formula =G4 * H3.

3. Press F4. Your formula should now look like this: =G4*$H$3.

Survival Tip On some keyboards you must press the Function key (which often has Fn or FN on it) and F4 to activate this combination.

4. Copy the formula from H4 down to H16. Ah, that's much better. Cell H16 now reads 130.

Of course, one of the beauties of this technique is that it makes it easier to update your numbers. For example, if you change 10% (in cell H3) to 20%, all your numbers change automatically. Yep, this is another sliver of Excel magic.

Note You can change this F4 configuration to fix a row instead of a cell in a formula (H$3) or fix a column ($H3), but this part of the book is meant to just give you enough to get going. You can see an example of fixing rows and fixing columns in the 01_Fixing_cells file, in the Fixing Rows sheet and the Fixing Columns sheet.

Rolling in the Worksheets

Most workbooks have multiple worksheets in them. Excel refers to worksheets interchangeably as *tabs* or *worksheets* or *sheets* (and I do, too). The following subsections provide quick reminders on how to handle a number of common tasks with worksheets.

Renaming a Sheet

To use either of the following methods, open a blank Excel workbook.

On the Sheet Tab

1. Double-click a name of the worksheet you want to rename. It becomes black.

2. Type a new name (e.g., Green) and press Enter. That's it!

With the Right-Click Menu

1. Right-click anywhere on the sheet you want to rename and select Rename (see Figure 1-9).

2. Type a new name (e.g., Green) into the sheet tab and press Enter.

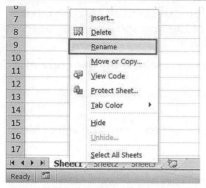

Figure 1-9

Moving a Sheet Within a Workbook

To try the following methods, you can continue with the workbook you have just been working with.

On the Sheet Tab

1. Hover the mouse over the sheet tab you want to move.

2. Press the left mouse button. You see a tiny black triangle appear to the left of the tab and a page appear at the end of your mouse pointer.

3. Keeping your left mouse button pressed down, drag the sheet to its new location and release the mouse.

With the Right-Click Menu

1. Right-click anywhere on the sheet you want to move and select Move or Copy (see Figure 1-10).

2. In the Move or Copy dialog, under Before Sheet, click the sheet that appears just before where you want to move the current sheet.

3. Click OK.

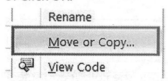

Figure 1-10

Copying a Sheet Within a Workbook

On the Sheet Tab

1. Hover the mouse over the sheet tab you wish to copy.

2. Simultaneously press and hold the left mouse button and the Ctrl key. A tiny black triangle appears to the left of the tab, and a page appears at the end of your mouse pointer, with + on it.

3. Keeping the left mouse button pressed down, drag the copy to its new location and release the mouse.

With the Right-Click Menu

1. Right-click anywhere on the sheet you want to move and select Move or Copy.

2. In the Move or Copy dialog, under Before Sheet, click the sheet that appears just before where you want to move the current sheet.

3. Select the Create a Copy check box (see Figure 1-11).

4. Click OK.

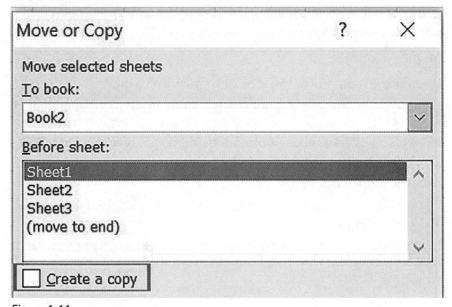

Figure 1-11

Colouring a Sheet

1. Right-click the sheet where you want to change the colour and select Tab Color.

2. Choose a colour from the palette (see Figure 1-12). The colour is changed, but you do not really see the change until you click on another worksheet and then return to the one with the changed colour.

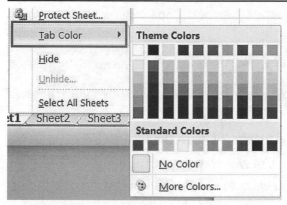

Figure 1-12

Deleting a Sheet

Note Be careful: This is one move in Excel that you can't undo.

1. Right-click the sheet you want to delete and select Delete (see Figure 1-13).

2. Click OK. If you have data in the sheet you are about to delete, Excel gives you a warning. Otherwise, it just deletes the sheet.

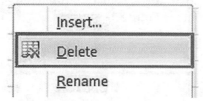

Figure 1-13

Moving a Sheet to Another Workbook

1. Ensure that the workbook to which you want to move a sheet is open.

2. Right-click the sheet you want to move to another workbook and select Move or Copy.

3. From the dropdown list in the Move or Copy dialog, choose the file you want to move the sheet to:

- If you want to move it into a brand-new workbook, choose (new book) from this dropdown.

- If you are moving it into an existing file, under Before Sheet, click the sheet that appears just before where you want to move the current sheet.

Then click OK. Excel moves the sheet, and it no longer exists in the original workbook.

> **Note** This technique is especially useful because if you just cut or copy and paste over data from one worksheet to another workbook, you lose a lot of the formatting (e.g., column widths). But if you move across a sheet this way, the formatting stays put.

Copying a Sheet to Another Workbook

1. Ensure that the workbook to which you want to copy a sheet is open.

2. Right-click the sheet you want to copy to another workbook and select Move or Copy.

3. Select the Create a Copy check box.

4. From the dropdown list in the Move or Copy dialog, choose the file you want to copy the sheet to:

- If you want to copy it into a brand-new workbook, choose (new book) from this dropdown.

- If you are copying it into an existing file, make sure you have selected the destination file in the dropdown list at the top and then, under Before Sheet, click the sheet that appears just before where you want to move the current sheet (see Figure 1-14).

5. Then click OK.

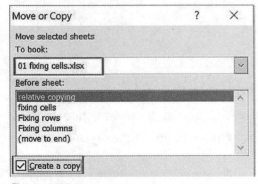

Figure 1-14

Printing in Excel

Please put down the scissors, staples, glue, and sticky tape and step away (slowly) from the photocopier. Something that comes up over and over again in classes I teach is the perennial problem of printing. Oh yes, I mention scissors, glue, and staples, and inevitably a few heads start to bob and wry smiles appear. Often when you print in Excel, what you want to print does not fit on the page—and the glue and scissors invariably get whipped out. (The cynic in me wonders if, in fact, the glue is needed after the stress of the entire process….) There's got to be a way around this, right? Right.

Well, the main thing you need to remember is that most of what you need for printing is available on the Page Layout tab (see Figure 1-15).

Figure 1-15

Fitting a Worksheet on a Printed Page

1. Open the file 01_Printing_sample.

2. View the file in Print Preview (either by selecting the view from the Quick Access toolbar) or by selecting File | Print. You can now see how the printed file will look, without actually having to send it to the printer. Notice that the file wants to print on 26 pages, and you are missing the heading ScdStartDate (see Figure 1-16).

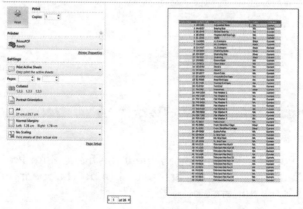

Figure 1-16

In fact, if you keep going through the pages, you will find that ScdStart-Date has decided to declare itself an independent republic and print itself on pages 15 onward. (You reached for your scissors, glue, and sticky tape, didn't you? Please put down all those implements quietly as you learn how to do this in a much easier way.)

3. To make everything fit on the printed page in this case, select the Page Layout tab and find the Width dropdown in the Scale to Fit options section (see Figure 1-17). In it select 1 page instead of Automatic.

4. Check the file in Print Preview. The document is now going to print on 11 pages, and ScdStartDate has rejoined its comrades, where it belongs. Magic!

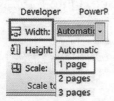

Figure 1-17

> **Note** If you have a document that will not fit tidily onto the desired number of pages, fix it with the Width option on the Page Layout tab.

Survival Tip To make a smaller spreadsheet appear bigger than it is, increase the % size in the Scale box on the Page Layout tab (see Figure 1-18).

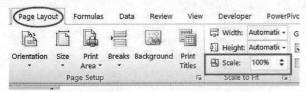

Figure 1-18

Printing Headings on Every Page: A Title! My Spreadsheet for a Title!

1. Keeping the file 01_Printing_sample open, view the file in Print Preview. Notice that headings appear on the first page but don't appear on the following pages. This is a nuisance.

2. Select Page Layout | Print Titles (see Figure 1-19).

Figure 1-19

3. In the Page Setup dialog that appears, click in the Rows to Repeat at Top box (see Figure 1-20).

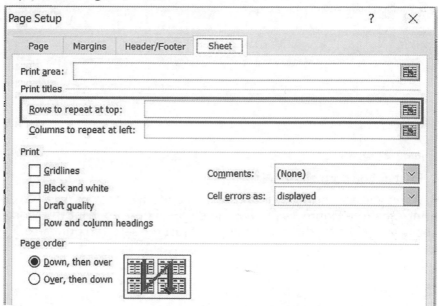

Figure 1-20

4. On the actual spreadsheet, click on the row number (on the left side of the screen) that has the headings you want to repeat at the top of every page; in this case, click row 1. You now see $1:$1 in the Rows to Repeat at Top box in the dialog.

5. Check the file in Print Preview again. The headings now appear at the top of every page.

> **Survival Tip** If you have a spreadsheet with multiple columns, and you want the first column to repeat on every page, choose Page Layout | Print Titles. Then select the Columns to Repeat at Left box and highlight the columns you want to appear on the left side of every page.

Printing Only Part of a Page

1. Highlight what you want to print and select Page Layout | Print Area | Set Print Area (see Figure 1-21).

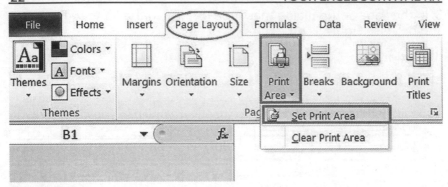

Figure 1-21

2. Print as you normally would.

3. When you are finished printing, select Page Layout | Print Area | Clear Print Area (see Figure 1-22). Next time you choose to print this worksheet, you will print the whole thing, not just the selected print area.

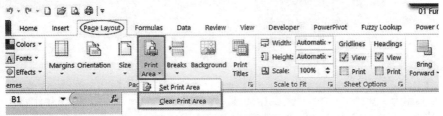

Figure 1-22

Note If you do not clear the print area, Excel prints out just this specific selection the next time you print the worksheet.

Changing the Page Orientation

1. To change the page orientation from Portrait to Landscape, select Page Layout | Orientation | Landscape.

2. To change the page orientation from Landscape to Portrait, select Page Layout | Orientation | Portrait (see Figure 1-23).

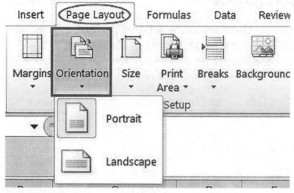

Figure 1-23

Inserting Page Breaks

Breaking up is not hard to do—for pages. Use the following steps when you need page breaks at points in a spreadsheet that Excel does not consider "natural" page breaks.

1. Click where you want a page break to go.

2. Select Page Layout | Breaks | Insert Page Break (see Figure 1-24). Yep, it's that simple.

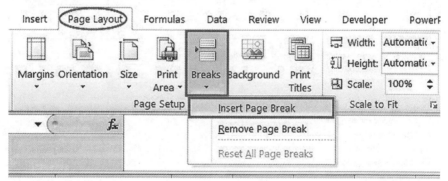

Figure 1-24

Removing Page Breaks

1. If you find that a page break doesn't work for you, click on the spread-sheet beside the break (or underneath, if it's a horizontal page break) and then select Page Layout | Breaks | Remove Page Break.

2. If you have inserted many page breaks and you now have no idea what is working or not, select Page Layout | Breaks | Reset All Page Breaks to restore the spreadsheet to its original, natural, page breaks.

Adding Headers and Footers

What if you want your name, the filename, a page number, or where you put the file to appear on every page? What if you want to make it clear that you *own* this spreadsheet? In this case, you add a header or footer—or both.

1. Select Page Layout | Print Titles (see Figure 1-25).

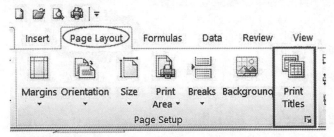

Figure 1-25

2. In the Page Setup dialog box that appears, select the Header/Footer tab (see Figure 1-26).

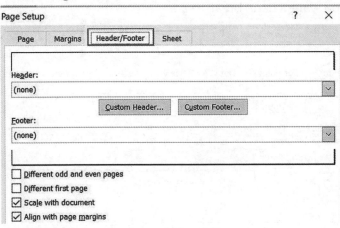

Figure 1-26

3. To make your name appear at the top of every page, choose an option from the dropdown list. You can choose from a number of choices, including filename and path, your name, and date (see Figure 1-27).

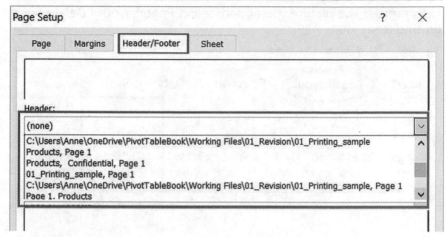

Figure 1-27

4. If you want the date to appear at the bottom of every page, choose Date from the Footer dropdown.

Adding a Picture in the Background

At some point you might want to add a favourite picture or motivational quote as a background to a spreadsheet. When you do this, the background picture doesn't actually print with your worksheet, but it does appear onscreen.

1. Select Page Layout | Background (see Figure 1-28).

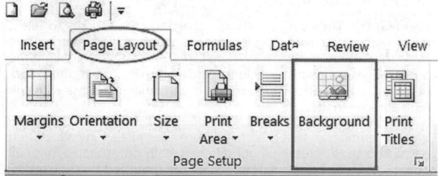

Figure 1-28

2. Browse to a folder where you have photos stored and select a photo.

3. Click OK. Your selected photo now appears as the background for the entire worksheet—all million-plus rows of it.

4. To remove the picture you added, select Page Layout | Delete Background (see Figure 1-29).

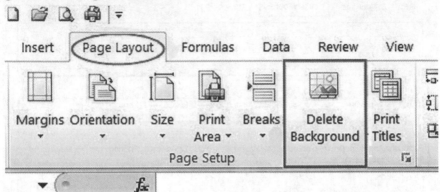

Figure 1-29

Charts, Charts, Charts

Rob Collie once observed in a blog post that Excel lovers tend to fall into two camps. One camp declares "I want a chart with that!" to everything. The other camp (the one I fall into, I confess) has a secret hankering for formulas and doesn't love charts so much. However, since most of the business world falls into the first camp, you need to be able to add at least basic charts to your spreadsheets.

The following sections cover creating basic column charts, pie charts, and combination charts.

> **Survival Tip** When you're making a chart, use the Ctrl key to select only the data you need. By this I mean highlight the first range. Then press the Ctrl key and, while keeping Ctrl pressed down, highlight the other ranges you want to include. Oddly enough, charts often work better if the top-left cell is blank; this is particularly the case with column and bar charts.

I want to emphasise that this chapter provides just an introduction to charts. Also, the approach I suggest here is really only suitable for smaller data sets. If you have much larger data sets, I suggest that you make a pivot table and then extract a pivot chart from it. (You'll learn about this in Chapter 5, "Creating Pivot Tables.")

Making a Basic Column Chart

1. Open the file 01_Chart_demo.

Survival Tip Think about exactly what you want your chart to show. (In this case, you want to make a column chart that shows the amount of money spent each day). Then make sure you highlight only the data you need. (In this case, you need just the Date and Amount columns.) Keep in mind that in some situations, you may need to use your Ctrl key to select only the data you need.

2. Click the Date heading and press Ctrl+Shift+Down Arrow to highlight the entire Date column.

3. With the Ctrl key pressed, click the Amount heading. While still holding down the Ctrl key, also press Shift+Down Arrow to select the Amount column in addition to the Date column.

4. Click Insert | Column and choose the first chart in the list—the clustered chart in the 2-D Column section (see Figure 1-30).

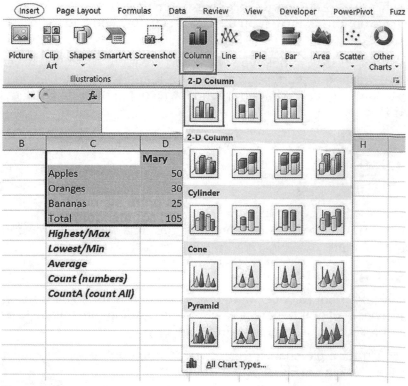

Figure 1-30

5. Release the mouse. That's it: Excel creates your column chart. Excel also gives you some new ribbon tabs at the top right of the screen: Design, Layout, and Format (see Figure 1-31).

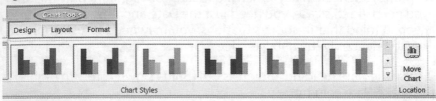

Figure 1-31

> **Survival Tips** Click on the Design tab and note that you have a veritable gallery of different chart types in the Chart Styles section. (At this point, be sure to pause to consider that you are now poised to join the pantheon of Excel gods and goddesses you have admired with their gee-whiz charts.) It is worthwhile to experiment a bit with them. You also have options to the left on the Design tab for changing the chart layout.
>
> Here's another trick to help you with chart creation: When you have finished creating a chart, you can click on it and then click Design | Switch Row/Column to change around the layout of the data (see Figure 1-32).

Figure 1-32

6. Practise creating another column chart, this time with the Payee and Amount columns.

Making a Pie Chart

It's really important to understand that a pie chart is suitable for showing just *one* set of numbers, ideally where the headings are unique (e.g., gender breakdown of employees in a company).

1. To construct a pie chart for category and amount, open the sheet called Pie Chart in the file 01_Chart_demo.

2. Highlight the headings in A1 and B1 and press Ctrl+Shift+Down Arrow to highlight all the headings and amounts.

3. Choose Insert | Pie | 2-D Pie | Pie (see Figure 1-33). Now you have a pie chart.

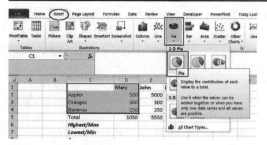

Figure 1-33

4. To add percentages to the pie chart, click on the chart and select De-sign | Chart Layouts (to the left of the Chart Styles) and select a layout, such as Chart Layout 1, which adds percentages and labels to your pie chart.

Making a Combination Chart

A combination chart includes two or more types of charts. A common type of combination chart is a column chart with a line in it to show something like targets. This chart type is beloved by many organisations, so it's useful to know how to make it.

Now, I'm going to be a bit unorthodox here in that there are better ways to create charts than the one I'm about to show you. But this book is not called *How to Be a Wonderful Chart Creator*. It's called *Excel Survival Guide*, and it's about ways to quickly get through typical Excel scenarios.

1. Open the Combination worksheet in the 01_Chart_demo file.

2. Assuming that you have set a daily total of 500, and you want that to appear as a line on your chart, add an extra column called Target that has 500 repeated all the way down (see Figure 1-34).

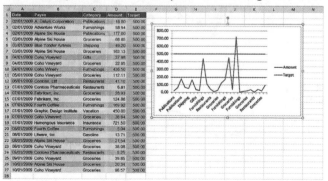

Figure 1-34

3. Highlight the three column headings Category, Amount, and Target and select Insert | Column | 2-D Column | Stacked Column (yep, living dangerously!).

4. To convert the Target part of the chart into a line chart, click one of the red columns. Note that small circles (I often call them Mickey Mouse ears) appear on all the red headings (see Figure 1-35). (If you're reading the print version of this book, I'm sorry to say you can't actually see the red colour. But trust me: It's there. And you can see the small circles in Figure 1-35.)

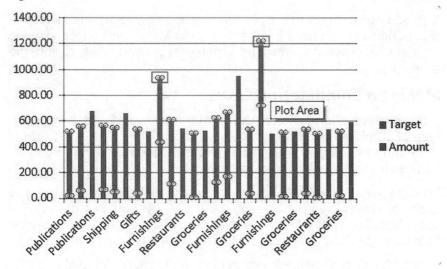

Figure 1-35

5. Select Design | Change Chart Type (see Figure 1-36).

Figure 1-36

6. Select Line | Line. You now have a horizontal line for your target.

> **Note** Jon Peltier (http://peltiertech.com) provides a much more comprehensive tutorial on creating a chart like this. In his version, the horizontal line actually stretches all the way across. However, as a first quick step, what I show here will get you started.

A Dirty Secret About Charts

I'm about to let you in on a dirty little secret about lines on charts. More than once people have admitted to me that they just *drew the line*. I know you want to know how to do this small cheat, so I'm going to tell you how:

1. It's easiest if you have gridlines on your chart, so make sure you have them by clicking on the chart and selecting Layout | Gridlines | Primary Horizontal Gridlines and clicking Major Gridlines.

2. Identify the point on the chart where you want the line to go. It's probably best to align the horizontal line with one of the gridlines.

3. Select Insert | Shapes and select a line type.

4. Click and drag the line across the chart. Hey, you have your line!

5. To change the colour of the line, click the line and select Format | Shape Outline and select a colour.

6. To change the weight of the line, select Format | Shape Outline | Weight and click the line with the desired thickness (e.g., 3pts).

Keyboard Navigation

Of course, before you complete this chapter, I need to mention keyboard shortcuts. An important part of using Excel effectively is having a repertoire of Excel shortcuts for navigating around. Here's how I recommend you build such a repertoire:

1. Choose one or two shortcuts a week, starting with shortcuts for stuff you do frequently, such as cutting and pasting (Ctrl+X and Ctrl+V) and inserting and removing columns (Ctrl++ and Ctrl+-)

2. Work on these new-to-you shortcuts all week, until by the end of the week they are in your muscle memory.

3. The following week, repeat steps 1 and 2 with a new set of shortcuts.

By the end of a couple of months, your speed and efficiency in navigating around Excel will have improved considerably.

Table 1-1 lists the most common Excel shortcuts. I've chosen these short-cuts because you will probably be working with large (thousands-plus) data sets, and if you do not use them, you will spend chunks of your life scrolling painstakingly down to the end of your sheet and then equally laboriously crawling to the top again—like someone coming up slowly from the bottom of the ocean.

Table 1-1: Excel Shortcuts

Shortcut	Description
Ctrl+Down Arrow	Moves to the bottom of the list (assuming no spaces)
Ctrl+Up Arrow	Moves to the top of the list (assuming no spaces)
Ctrl+Right Arrow	Moves to the extreme right of the list (assuming no spaces)
Ctrl+Left Arrow	Moves to the extreme left of the list (assuming no spaces)
Ctrl+Shift+*	Selects the entire list (Thanks to Chandoo at http://chandoo.org for this one!)
Ctrl+Home	Moves to A1 from anywhere in the spreadsheet
Ctrl+End	Moves to last cell clicked in the spreadsheet (like moving to the furthest footprint on newly fallen snow)

Of course you can find many more keyboard shortcuts at the Microsoft site.

Summary

This chapter covers the basics of Excel: data entry, formulas, fixing cells, printing, charts, and worksheet housekeeping. If you can do this much with speed and grace, you are already ahead of many Excel users. Knowing this stuff will make you a hardy Excel survivor. If you continue through the following chapters, you will become an Excel thriver.

Chapter 2 Getting Your Data Together: Catching Your File

At this point, you have some basic Excel survival skills. You have revisited how to make basic formulas, how to print, and how to create a chart, and you have started learning Excel shortcuts. In many ways, you are already ahead of the crowd. Now it's time to learn about normalizing data, which becomes especially crucial when you want to use pivot tables. (And you will want to use them! As you'll learn in Chapter 5, "Creating Pivot Tables," they make your life much easier!)

In some ways, this is the most important chapter of the book. Many Excel users try to work with data that is not normalized, and they have a lot of problems because of that. It is beyond the scope of this book to go into the full intricacies of normalization, but you can read the basics according to Wikipedia (https://en.wikipedia.org/wiki/Database_normalization) and according to Microsoft (https://support.microsoft.com/en-us/kb/283878). Basically, for Excel purposes, *normalization* means having your data organized in a list, following certain guidelines. (Don't worry: I will mention these guidelines a few times in this chapter.)

> **Note** If you are pulling data from an external source, which is also known rather inelegantly as a "data dump," the data is probably already normalized. The rules for normalizing your data will therefore be most important to you when you are capturing data as you go along.

Often the end goal with an Excel file is to create a pivot table from it, which essentially means using Excel to summarize large data sets based on various fields (e.g., months, regions). As a student once said to me, the world of work runs on two things: pivot tables and PowerPoint.

Before you can create a pivot table, you need to make sure your data is normalized and in table format. You'll learn how to do both of those things in this book. You may be feeling exhausted already, just thinking about all this work, but it's okay: You can do this.

When you are creating an Excel file, you generally have two choices:

- Choice 1: Create a spreadsheet list from scratch.
- Choice 2: Get data from a data dump (i.e., pull in the data from another program).

Both choices have their own unique challenges, and we'll get into all of them in this chapter.

Creating a Spreadsheet List from Scratch

There are a couple of things to consider when you are creating a spreadsheet list from scratch:

- Is this just a simple list (e.g., names, addresses, phone numbers)? If so, you can create a simple list.

- Is this a list of recurring items (e.g., training, with the same person doing many different courses on different dates)? If so, you can create a recurring list.

These two approaches are a bit different, as you'll see in the following sections.

Creating a Simple List

I suggest the approach described in this section because I assume that you are probably going to want to sort your list alphabetically at some stage and are going to need to look for specific information. I'm guessing here, but you are probably not going to spend a morning (or an afternoon) just reading your entire list for pleasure.

> **Note** I got the names in the file 02_Simple_list from the very useful site www.fakenamegenerator.com.

To create a simple list, you need to start by getting a solid idea of the data you want to include in your list (e.g., first name, surname, phone number). Then you create headings across the top of a worksheet, one heading per cell, with no blank columns in between. Unless you think you are never going to sort by surname, put first name and surname in separate cells.

To see how to create a simple list, follow these steps to add the titles across the top of your worksheet and then add two entries:

1. In cell A1, type `Title`.

2. In cell B1, type `GivenName`.

3. In cell C1, type `Surname`.

4. In cell D1, type `StreetAddress`.

5. In cell E1, type `City`.

6. In cell F1, type `Emailaddress`.

7. In cell G1, type `Telephone number`.

8. Highlight cells A1 to G1 and make them bold. (This tells Excel that these entries are to be treated as headings.)

9. In cell A2, type `Mrs.`

10. In cell B2, type `Savanna.`

11. In cell C2, type `Greenhand.`

12. In cell D2, type `39 Brackley Road.`

13. In cell E2, type `THWAITE.`

14. In cell F2, type `SavannaGreenhand@dayrep.com.`

15. In cell G2, type `077 8782 7374.`

> **Note** If you are entering phone numbers, either prefix them with an apostrophe (`'`) or format the entire column as text (by highlighting the column and selecting Text from the dropdown in the Number group of the Home tab, as shown in Figure 2-1). This ensures that leading zeros are maintained, so that if you enter, for example, 077 8782 7374, you will see 077 8782 7374 and not 77 8782 7374).

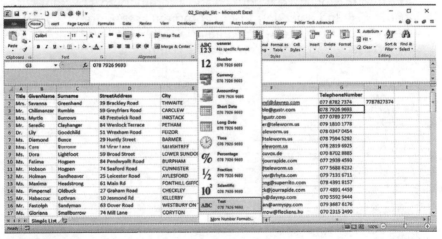

Figure 2-1

16. In cell A3, type `Mr..`

17. In cell B3, type `Chilimanzar.`

18. In cell C3, type `Rumble.`

19. In cell D3, type `59 Greyfriars Road.`

20. In cell E3, type `CARCLEW.`

21. In cell F3, type `ChilimanzarRumble@gustr.com.`

22. In cell G3, type `078 7926 9693.`

You can see the finished list in the file 02_Simple_list. Notice that there are no blank rows or columns in the list.

Some Observations About Data Entry

Be consistent with your repeated entries. For example, in the simple list in the preceding section, you entered THWAITE as a town in cell E2. If you check cell E7 and cell E15 in the file 02_Simple_list, you see that it has been entered in those cells in exactly the same way. As described later in this chapter, you can use a validation list (a dropdown list from which the user can select an item) to ensure accurate data entry.

Why is consistent data entry important? If you are looking for lists of people in THWAITE, Excel will treat THWAITE, THWAITE TOWN, and City of THWAITE as three different places. Yes, you know they are all the same place, but Excel doesn't. To avoid confusing Excel, follow these guidelines:

- Ensure that the only entries in a column belong there. For example, the Surname column should contain only, yes, surnames. To provide more information in a cell, you can add a comment to it by right-clicking the cell and selecting Insert Comment (see Figure 2-2). Then, when you click on a cell that contains a comment (which now has a tiny red marker on it), you can read the comment.

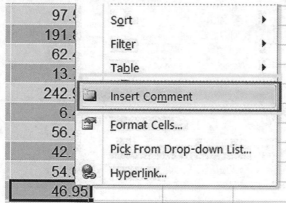

Figure 2-2

- Don't mix dates and text and numbers in the same cell. Doing so is like mixing water and oil: It just doesn't work.
- In date columns, make sure you have a date entry in each cell. If you try to use a pivot table for analysis later on, Excel will choke if it encounters any blank dates. If a particular cell doesn't need a date, just enter the first or last entry for the month.

As you keep adding to your list, be sure to follow the data entry rules mentioned so far.

Survival Tip Keep in mind these principles as you create simple lists:

- No blank rows / No blank columns
- Bold headings
- One heading in each cell
- Validation lists for repeating data (e.g., departments, course names)

Creating a Validation List

If you have repeating data (e.g., training course name, county, department), I strongly advise using validation lists. A *validation list* is simply a dropdown list which ensures that users always enter data in a consistent way. A validation list can also prevent people from entering data in any undesired formats (e.g., THWAITE TOWN or City of THWAITE instead of THWAITE).

> **Note** Although the validation list you will build here is shown with a simple list, you can also use validation lists to create more complex recurring lists, as discussed later in the chapter.

1. Open a new workbook.

2. Name one of the sheets Lists.

3. Name another sheet Data.

4. Move to the Lists sheet.

5. In cell D5, type `Dwarf`.

6. In cell D6, type `Elf`.

7. In cell D7, type `Ent`.

8. In cell D8, type `Hobbit`.

9. In cell D9, type `Orc`.

10. Highlight all five of these cells (D5:D9)

11. Click Insert | Table (see Figure 2-3). In the dialog box that appears, leave the My Table Has Headers check box unticked (see Figure 2-4).

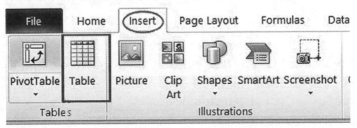

Figure 2-3

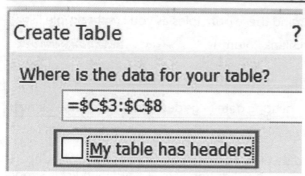

Create Table   ?

Where is the data for your table?

=$C$3:$C$8

☐ **My table has headers**

Figure 2-4

12. Click OK.

13. Click on the list and then, on the Design tab, remove the check from Header Row (to prevent Excel from including the title of the list or the heading Column1 in the dropdown).

14. Highlight the list again and make it a named range by clicking in the Name box on the left and typing the name Position (see Figure 2-5). Press Enter.

Position	▼		f_x		
	A	B	C	D	E	F
1						
2						

Figure 2-5

Note Spaces are not allowed in range names.

You have just created the data source for your validation list. In this case, you made the list a table because if you need to add another position later, your validation list will automatically update to include the new name when you add it to the table.

Adding the Data Validation List to the Data Sheet

1. Move to the worksheet called Data, which is where you are going to create a validation list for entering positions.

2. In cell C3, type Position as a heading.

3. Highlight the range C24:C28.

4. Select Data | Data Validation | Data Validation (see Figure 2-6).

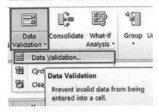

Figure 2-6

5. In the Data Validation dialog that appears, click the Settings tab and choose List under the Allow box.

6. Click in the Source box and press F3 to bring up your list of range names.

7. Click the range name Position and then click OK. Now when the user clicks in cell C4, he or she can select a name from the dropdown list. The user can choose any one of the dropdown options but cannot choose multiple positions at once and cannot enter anything that's not on this list (e.g., Wizard).

> **Survival Tips** You can sort this dropdown list into alphabetical order by clicking in the table in the Data sheet, right-clicking, and selecting Sort | Sort A to Z.
>
> Also, sometimes Excel does not pick up the named range, and you may have to select the data you have created for your list or re-create the range name.

> **Note** Because you used a table for your data validation list, you can very easily add new items to that list. For example, if you now return to the Lists sheet and type in `Wizard` in cell D10, the validation list is automatically updated.

Adding an Input Message and an Error Alert

1. On the Data worksheet, highlight the area where you have applied the validation list.

2. Select Data | Data Validation | Data Validation.

3. In the Data Validation dialog that appears, select the Input tab, click in the Input Message box, and type the message you want to appear when someone hovers his or her mouse on this dropdown list (e.g., `Please choose an item from the list`).

4. Still in the Data Validation dialog box, click on Error Alert and type an appropriate message (e.g., `What part of pick from the list don't you understand?` or something more polite) in the Error

Message box. This is a way to administer a virtual rap on the knuckles to anyone who dares to choose something not on the list.

> **Note** The file 02_Data_entry_recurring_list shows this valida-tion list as well as lists for the other headings in the Data sheet (Status, Department, and Course Attended).

> **Note** In Excel when you use a table as the source for a vali-dation list, you can only have *one* column in that table. Excel doesn't allow the use of two or more columns in a table used for data validation.

Converting a List to a Table

It is a good idea to convert a simple or recurring list (as on the Data sheet in the file 02_Data_entry_recurring_list) to a table when you have finished creating all your dropdown lists.

1. Click anywhere in the list and press Ctrl+T (or select Insert | Table).

2. In the Create Table dialog box that appears, click OK. Excel indicates the range to be included in the table (e.g., =$A$3:$H$28 if that is the range highlighted).

Figuring Out Which Columns Have Data Validation Lists

1. In a worksheet where you don't know what columns have data valida-tion applied, press F5 and select Special | Data Validation.

2. Click OK. The cells that have data validation applied are now high-lighted.

For more data validation techniques, see this book's Appendix, page 159, "Data Validation Techniques."

Creating a Recurring List

We have just spent some time looking at creating simple lists. However, a more common scenario is capturing recurring data—such as training records, where the same people will be attending different courses at different times or the same course at different times. In this situation, you have to track who attended what and where and when. You might also need to issue different invoices to the same customer.

Both of the scenarios just described involve capturing recurring infor-mation. Excel users often expend a lot of unnecessary effort setting up and dealing with this sort of data collection. But there's a way to set up your data in Excel that makes it a snap to manage. This approach is very similar to what you have just done with a simple list, but now you must record every part of the transaction separately (i.e., if an invoice has many products, there must be a line for every product—even if it's from the same invoice). The same goes for capturing training records: All details must be recorded every time.

Inexperienced users often record their data in a pivot table–like layout, as shown in Table 2-1.

Table 2-1: Non-normalized Data: *DON'T SET UP YOUR DATA LIKE THIS! TRUST ME, DON'T!*

	USA	Ireland	UK	France	Germany	Japan
Customer A	100	200	300	400	500	600
Customer B	600	300	400	500	200	100
Customer C	1000	800	750	450	900	1000

If you set up your data this way, you're likely to need to pull an all-nighter or work all week to make it happen. Then next month you'll be asked to present the same data in a different format, such as total by month by country. Or you will get a new customer or a new country. And then you'll have to go back to square one. And this will keep happening—every month. This is the sort of stuff that gets Excel a really bad name. But it doesn't have to be this way!

You can avoid all this pain if you ensure that the data is normalized. If you set up your data in a normalized fashion, it will be much easier to slice and dice the data in all sorts of ways with a pivot table.

Brief Introduction to Normalization

As mentioned earlier in this chapter, for Excel purposes, *normalization* means having your data organized in a list, following certain guidelines. You should enter your data row by row, with each row containing full details of the transaction.

To the inexperienced eye, normalized data entry can look very repetitive, and many are tempted to go straight into putting data in a pivot format (as shown above)—but I repeat, don't do it! You may save some time in the short run, but you will end up doing a great deal of totally unnecessary work.

Here is the basic guideline for entering normalized data: Enter every entry (or *record*) as if you are doing so for the first time—that is, as if you are recording all the relevant data for your first record. Table 2-2 shows what it should look like; note that this is the same data shown in Table 2-1, but now it is normalized—and therefore very usable. If you follow this simple rule, your data will be normalized, and when you have data like this, you can very easily use a pivot table (as described in Chapter 5) to get any analysis your boss requires.

> **Survival Tip** Enter every record as if you are doing so for the first time—that is, as if you are recording all the relevant data for your first record.

Table 2-2: Normalized Data

Customer	Country	Amount
Customer A	United States	100
Customer A	Ireland	200
Customer A	United Kingdom	300
Customer A	France	400
Customer A	Germany	500
Customer A	Japan	600
Customer B	United States	600
Customer B	Ireland	300
Customer B	United Kingdom	400
Customer B	France	500
Customer B	Germany	200
Customer B	Japan	100
Customer C	United States	1000
Customer C	Ireland	800
Customer C	United Kingdom	750
Customer C	France	450
Customer C	Germany	900
Customer C	Japan	1000

When you use this method, you have a single data sheet and can just keep adding records as you go along. As you can see, by doing it this way, you don't need to worry if a new customer or country is added: You just add it as a new row to your list.

This is how you need to set up your data in Excel. It may seem like *so much work*! Yes, it is, but once you have your data set up in this way, you can easily use a pivot table to extract analyses from it in moments.

> **Survival Tip** As you enter your data, remember that every entry should feel like the first time. (*Foreigner* had a rather fine ballad about this, although I'm pretty sure they weren't talking about Excel.)

You can see an example of this sort of list in the file 02_Data_entry_recurring_list. You can see there that the same people have taken many different courses, and their full names and details are entered every time.

Using validation lists, as discussed earlier in this chapter, can help you further cut down on your data entry work. In addition, if you use Vlookup()s (covered in Chapter 4, "The Vlookup() Function: An Excel Essential"), you can quickly enter data that doesn't change (e.g., date of birth).

> **Survival Tip** The same principles apply to creating recurring lists as to creating simple lists:
> - No blank rows / No blank columns
> - Bold headings
> - One heading in each cell
> - Validation lists for repeating data (e.g., departments, course names)

It is very likely that you will inherit files that are not normalized at all. Even though you didn't create those messes, you need to clean them up—if you want to be able to easily summarize and analyse your data. You can do this normalization manually, or you can use Power Query, a free add-in that allows you to normalize data much more easily. This book's Appendix describes some manual normalizing techniques, and Chapter 6, "Using Power Query to Quickly Clean Up Data," discusses Power Query.

Taking Advantage of Tables

You briefly met tables earlier in this chapter, when you created a validation list. This section digs a bit deeper into what tables can do for you.

A big recent development in the world of Excel is the expansion of the list feature (which is what tables were called in Excel 2003 and earlier) into tables. By using a table, you can enter one formula and have Excel automatically populate the rest of the cells in that column with the formula and format your data in a very presentable alternating colour format. After that, if you decide to "de-table" your data (i.e., convert it to a range), the formatting still remains.

Note You can see an example of a table in the file 02_Table_practice.

Using Structural References with Tables

Also, when you create a table (by pressing Ctrl+T), you can use *structural references*; this means that instead of referencing a specific cell by name (e.g., E2 in Prepared Table sheet in the 02_Table_practice file), you reference the column name (e.g., [Amount]). Also, if you reference a table when you are using pivot tables, Excel automatically makes the range dynamic so that all you need to do is refresh the data instead of having to reselect the data source all over. (See Chapter 5 for much more on pivot tables.)

Similarly, if you reference a table in a formula and then more data is added to the table, the formula automatically updates to include the new data. However, when you are creating the formula, you must use the table name and then the heading. For example, if you wanted to use a structural reference formula to get the total amount in the Prepared Table sheet of the 02_Table_practice file, this is how you would do it.

1. In cell H1, type =Sum(t.

2. From the list that pops up, select Table1 (the default name assigned to the table), as shown in Figure 2-7.

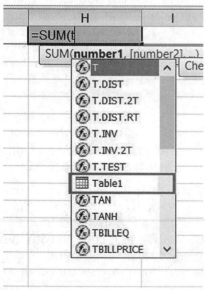

Figure 2-7

3. Type [, and in the list of headings that appears, click Amount.

4. Type] and press Enter. You should now see 57170 in cell H1.

5. Go down to the end of the table and enter 1000 in cell E926. The result of the formula you entered now updates automatically to 58170.

> **Note** Using a table in a formula can often make the formula easier to read. However, one drawback is that you must use the same formula all the way down a column, so you can't have a formula that says [@Amount] * 10% in one cell and then [@ Amount] / 10% in another.

When you create a table, Excel adds the Design tab to the ribbon (see Figure 2-8), which disappears when you click outside the table. You can use the Design tab to add and remove header cells and to add and remove totals.

Figure 2-8

Entering Data in a Table

1. Open the file 02_Table_practice and go to the Table Practice sheet.

2. Convert a list to a table by clicking anywhere in the list in A2:A29, selecting Insert | Table, and clicking OK. Your sheet starts to look prettier immediately.

3. Enter `Music Streaming` in cell A30 and notice that the table formatting automatically extends to include it. As you add other new entries at the end of the table, Excel automatically updates your table to include them.

4. Move to the Simple Table Practice sheet in the 02_Table_practice file.

5. Click anywhere in the sheet and notice a couple of things about your table at this point:

- You now have a filter dropdown beside each of your headings (which makes it easier to find data in the table).

- When you scroll down the list of data, the table headings appear in the column headings, which makes data entry easier.

Creating Formulas Using Structural References

One of the big advantages of using tables that you can't see at a glance is the use of structural references in formula creation.

1. In the Table Practice sheet of the 02_Table_practice file, click in cell F1 and type Profit. The column automatically formats itself so that it now becomes part of the table as well.

2. Click in cell F2, where you want to enter a formula that is going to show 10% of the amount. (Note that 10% has already been entered in H1.)

3. To enter the formula, type = and then click in E2. Note that what appears in your formula is [@Amount], not E2. This is the structural reference.

4. Complete the formula by typing * H1 while pressing F4 (to get the dollar signs). Your formula should now read =[@Amount]*$H$1.

5. Press Enter, and the rest of the formula is automatically filled in.

Structural references are hugely useful if you have large data sets because when you enter the formula into the first cell, it is copied down automatically to all the cells underneath. Imagine how helpful this is when you have thousands of rows!

> **Note** One limitation with structural references is that you can have only one formula in any table column.

> **Note** This section describes a typical scenario with recurring data, but sometimes you may need to create data in a different format. For example, you may need to use a different format for cash flow statements. You can see an example of that in the file 02_Cash_flow_statement.

Getting Data from a Data Dump

In many cases, you get data from an external source. A favourite joke in the Excel world is that the most used button in IT—after OK and Cancel—is Send to Excel. If you get data from an external source, you are quite familiar with this button.

Data is increasingly coming from ERP systems such as Oracle or JD Edwards. Usually you need to follow three basic steps with such data:

1. Identify what data you need from the source.

2. Get this data from the source.

3. Pull this data into Excel.

How you get the data from the source varies greatly from system to system, so we don't talk here about exactly how to do that. However, it is often in CSV (comma-separated values) format or text format, though you can often indicate that you want your data to come in as Excel.

The plus side of pulling in data from an external source is that it is *usually* already normalized. However, that is not always true for data dumps from accounting systems, which usually have lots of spaces, blank columns, and rows. (You'll learn more about easily cleaning up such data dumps in Chapter 6.)

Pulling In Data in CSV/Text Format

Once you have decided what you want to pull into Excel, the next step is to get it there. Usually, data from external sources is saved as text (.txt) or comma-separated values (.csv), so you usually need to go through a few steps before you can get the data into Excel. There are two main approaches:

- Open a saved text/CSV file
- Pull the data directly into Excel.

The following sections walk you through these two approaches.

Opening a Saved Text/CSV File

It is very common to pull data into Excel only as a CSV or text file. When you do this, you need to save your file as an Excel file in order to be able to use the full capabilities of Excel. When you open up a saved text file, the Text to Columns Wizard is usually triggered. To see how you use this wizard, follow these steps:

1. Open the file 02_Text_to_columns. If you don't see it in the list, as shown in Figure 2-9, change the dropdown that says All Excel Files to All Files so that Excel can "see" your text file.

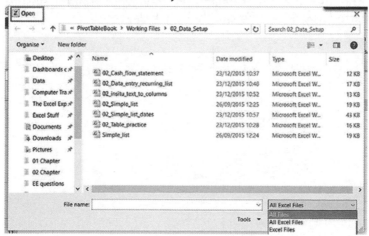

Figure 2-9

2. Click Open. You now see the dialog box shown in Figure 2-10.

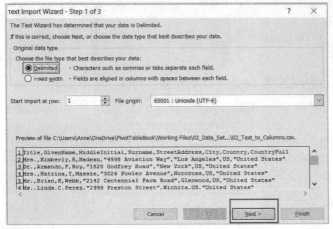

Figure 2-10

3. In the Step 1 of 3 dialog, choose how you want to divide up the data. The usual selection is Delimited (i.e., the data is separated by spaces/ commas, etc.), but sometimes you may need to use Fixed Width (for example, if you are dealing with names that have three parts each) to indicate where you want the divisions to be.

4. Choose a value in the Start Import at Row box. It's often easier just to accept what Excel suggests.

5. Click Next.

6. In the Step 2 of 3 dialog (see Figure 2-11), select Commas to indicate that you want to use commas as delimiters. Preview the data to ensure that it's formatted as you require and then click Next.

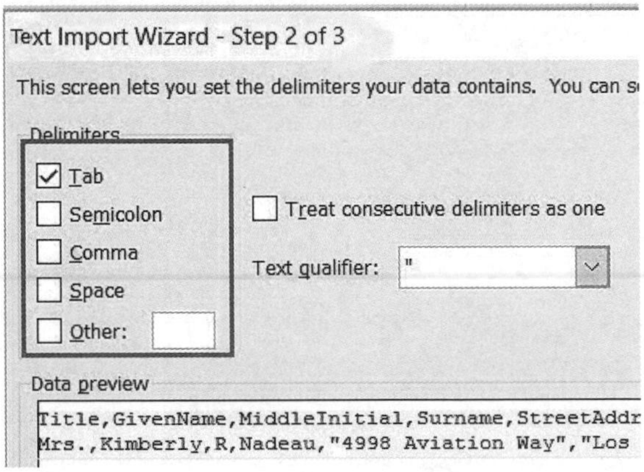

Figure 2-11

Note If you have multiple commas or other delimiters (which is common in downloads from accounting systems), select the Other box and enter the multiple delimiters after it. Then tick the Treat Consecutive Delimiters as One box to remove the extra commas. The beauty of doing this is that it eliminates the extra rows that Excel creates when it finds extra commas. However, this doesn't always work. Chapter 6 discusses some ways to get around that.

7. In the Step 3 of 3 dialog, choose General to import text as text, dates as dates, and numbers as numbers. Click Finish, and Excel imports the data.

Separating Data in Situ So the Imported Data Comes Straight into an Excel Sheet

Sometimes data comes into Excel without being separated out into its appropriate headings. For example, you may have names and addresses pulled into one cell instead of being separated out into separate cells. Or you may have data import as the incorrect format (e.g., numbers come in as text or vice versa). Here's how you deal with such problems:

1. Open the file 02_Insitu_text_to_columns, which shows all the entries in one cell.

2. Highlight column A and select Data | Text to Columns. The Text to Columns Wizard appears.

Survival Tip You can use the Text to Columns Wizard on only one column at a time.

3. In the Step 1 of 3 dialog, choose how you want to divide up the data. The usual selection is Delimited (i.e., the data is separated by spaces/commas, etc.), but sometimes you may need to use Fixed Width (for example, if you are dealing with names that have three parts each) to indicate where you want the divisions to be.

4. Choose a value in the Start Import at Row box.

5. Click Next.

6. In the Step 2 of 3 dialog, select Commas to indicate that you want to use commas as delimiters. Preview the data to ensure that it's formatted as you require and then click Next.

7. In the Step 3 of 3 dialog (see Figure 2-12), you now get the Destination option, which is by default the top cell of the column you have selected. If you want the data to go elsewhere (e.g., D2), click the icon on the right of the Destination box and select cell D2. (Or simply type $D$2 in the Destination box.) Click Finish.

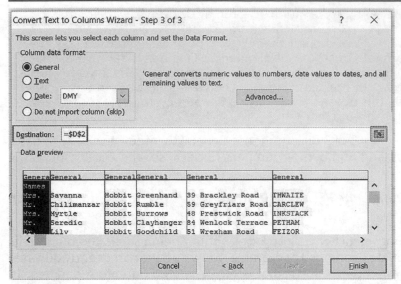

Figure 2-12

> **Note** If you use the Text to Columns Wizard in an existing list,
> you overwrite the contents of the columns to the right. So if
> your data is divided into three columns, the new data will over-
> write the contents of the data in the three columns immediate-
> ly to the right of your column. However, you will be prompted
> with the question "Do you want to replace the contents of the
> destination cells?" If you don't, you can insert extra columns by
> highlighting the column to the right and then selecting Home |
> Insert | Insert Sheet Columns (see Figure 2-13).

Figure 2-13

Other Uses for the Text to Columns Wizard

"I see dead numbers....Excel sees text."

Sometimes when you pull in data from an external data source for comparison purposes, Excel pulls in text entries as numbers or number entries as text. This is a problem if you need to use those cells in formulas.
For example, if you try to add up entries and Excel thinks they are text,

you may get an error instead of an answer. So you need to be able to import text as text, dates as dates, and numbers as numbers. Using the Text to Columns Wizard is one effective way to do that.

You may not be sure whether Excel is identifying your entries as text or numbers. One consideration is that Excel formats text on the left and numbers on the right. In addition, you can find out whether Excel is reading data as text or numbers by highlighting the data in question and looking at the Number box on the Home tab. For example, Figure 2-14 shows that Excel is reading some data as dates.

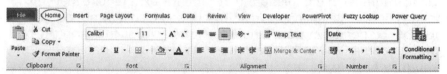

Figure 2-14

How do you tell Excel to use the data type you want? Sometimes it's just enough to highlight one of the data sets and convert it to the appropriate data type. But often, that's not enough. In such a case, you can highlight the data whose format you want to change and select Data | Text to Columns. If you are using Vlookup()s with this data (see Chapter 5)—or, indeed, most lookup-type functions, Excel returns an error message if the two sets of data do not have the same data type—even if they look exactly the same.

Another issue happens when data is a number that you want presented as text. For example, say you have a spare part number or a number that has leading zeros (e.g., 098766), and all you need it for is reference, so it's fine if it's text, but Excel keeps parking a green "yoke" (to use an Irish phrase for anything that doesn't lend itself to an easy description) in the top-left corner, earnestly and diligently warning you that it's a number. When you click it, you see a yellow marker and are prompted that it's a "number as text." You can then choose to click Ignore Error to remove it.

> **Survival Tip** Again, don't forget to make sure your data meets the following criteria:
>
> - No blank rows
> - No blank columns
> - Bold headings
> - One heading in each cell
> - Validation lists for repeating data (e.g., departments, course names)

Getting Data from a PDF into Excel

At this writing, there isn't a huge amount of really effective software for extracting data from a PDF file into Excel. The best of what is out there is NitroPDF, also called GoNitro (see www.gonitro.com). Another solution I have seen recommended is Able2Extract (see www.investintech.com/able2extract.html). But this is a constantly evolving field, and there may be many more options available by the time you read this.

Quite a number of the solutions that currently exist require that you upload your PDF file to an external site, but doing so may not be suitable for your corporate environment. When faced with such a problem, people sometimes manually type in the data from a PDF, and occasionally you may have to do that. However, in the meantime, there are some workarounds, as described in the following sections.

Option 1: Importing Directly into Excel

This option works only if your version of Adobe allows you to copy. Even if you can use this option, know that it is not pretty and leaves you with a lot of clean-up to do.

1. Copy and paste the data from the PDF into an Excel spreadsheet.

2. Select Data | Text to Columns and separate the data into the appropriate columns.

Option 2: Importing via Word

This option works only if your version of Adobe allows you to copy.

1. Copy and paste the data from the PDF into a Word document.

2. Copy and paste the data from the Word document into an Excel spreadsheet.

3. Highlight the column that contains the data.

4. Select Data | Text to Columns and separate the data into the appropriate columns.

5. In the Step 1 of 3 dialog, click Delimited and then click Next.

6. In the Step 2 of 3 dialog, tick the box for Comma and then click Next.

7. In the Step 3 of 3 dialog, tick the box for General and in the Destination box, enter the cell where you want the text to begin or accept the default and then click Finish.

Sorting and Filtering

Once your data is all set up and you can easily work with it, you're ready to tackle sorting and filtering in order to extract data that meets certain criteria.

Sorting

You can sort either by a single column or by multiple columns.

Follow these steps to sort one column from A to Z:

1. Reopen the file 02_Simple_list.

2. Right-click in the City column and select Sort | Sort A to Z (see Figure 2-15).

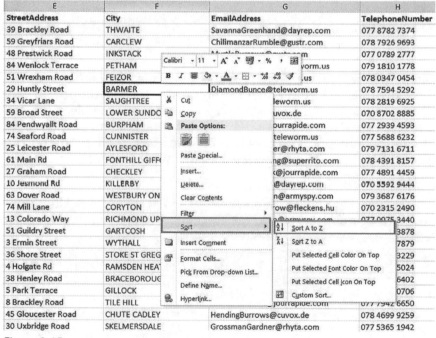

Figure 2-15

Follow these steps to sort multiple columns:

1. In the file 02_Simple_list, click anywhere in the list and select Data | Sort.

2. In the Sort dialog that appears, select the first column you want to sort by (e.g., Surname) under Column Sort By.

3. Click Add Level (see Figure 2-16) and then from the Then By drop-down list, choose the next heading you want to sort it by (e.g., City).

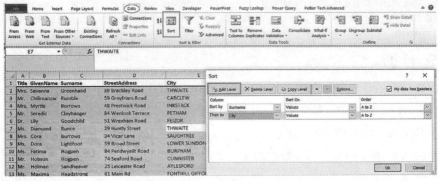

Figure 2-16

You can sort by up to 27 (!) levels.

Filtering

Filtering allows you to search for and show specific data. One of the great things about Excel is that the options in the filter dropdown vary depending on the type of data in the column. For example, if the column contains dates, the filter dropdown for that column provides a list of date options, and if the column contains text, the filter dropdown gives text options. To see how it works, follow these steps:

1. Open the file 02_Simple_list_dates.

2. Click anywhere in the list and select Data | Filter. A grey filter drop-down triangle appears beside each heading (see Figure 2-17).

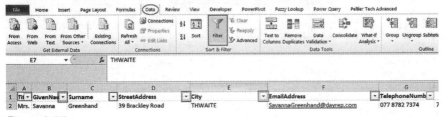

Figure 2-17

3. Click on one of the grey triangles and select the appropriate kind of filter. For example, if you click on the filter triangle beside Date, you see the options shown in Figure 2-18. The filters available here reflect the fact that the entries in this column are dates. You can choose, for example, to include only certain months or certain date ranges by selecting Date Filters | Before.

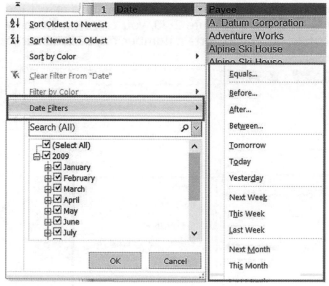

Figure 2-18

4. Click the filter triangle beside Payee, and your filter options are text based. As shown in Figure 2-19, you can choose to filter by a specific entry (e.g., Adventure Works) or by entries with specific text (e.g., Text Filters | Contains | Type in Adventure).

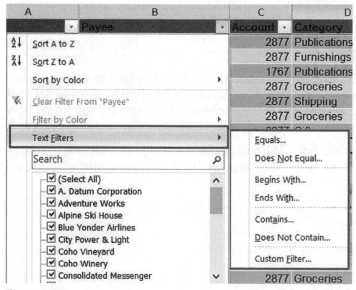

Figure 2-19

5. Click the filter triangle beside Amount, your filter options reflect the numbers in this list. As shown in Figure 2-20, you can filter to show amounts greater than or less than a certain number, or you can filter to show the top 10.

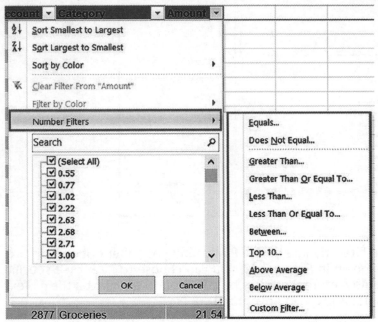

Figure 2-20

Summary

This is probably one of the most important chapters in this book because the vast majority of problems in Excel happen because a data set is not normalized. But *you* are now ahead of the crowd. You know how to set up your data for ease and success with Excel.

In this chapter you have learned about creating lists, setting up drop-down lists for data validation, applying tables to data, and sorting and filtering.

Survival Tip I'll say it one more time....Ensure that your data meets the following criteria:

- No blank rows / No blank columns
- Bold headings
- One heading in each cell
- Validation lists for repeating data (e.g., departments, course names)

Chapter 3 Further Cleaning, Slicing, and Dicing

Say that at this point you have your data in a spreadsheet. It's getting tidy and taking shape, but you still need to do some more clean-up. This chapter covers the techniques most commonly used to organise, manipulate, and prepare data. It is not intended to cover every possible technique, but it does address the issues I have heard the most confusion about in classes, including the following:

- Removing/completing blank rows/columns/cells
- Cleaning, combining, and amending existing data
- Extracting specific pieces of data from a cell to help refine the data set

Removing/Completing Blank Columns/Rows/Cells

Remember that the Holy Grail in terms of Excel data is a normalized list with no blank rows and no blank columns. The following sections show how to fix problems related to blank columns, rows, and cells.

Removing Blank Columns/Rows

1. Open the file 03_Blank_rows_columns.

2. To delete one blank column at a time, highlighting the column heading, right-click, and select Delete.

3. To delete multiple columns at once, highlight the first column (e.g., D). Then hold down the Ctrl key and highlight the other columns you want to remove (e.g., G and J) and press Ctrl+– (minus).

Follow the same steps to delete unwanted blank rows but (obviously) select the blank rows rather than blank columns. In the file 03_Blank_rows_columns, the blank rows are 12, 23, and 37.

Completing Blank Cells

Sometimes you need to quickly enter the same data (e.g., 0) into all blank cells. The following is a useful technique for quickly doing that.

1. Open the file 03_Blank_cells.

2. Highlight the data set that includes blank cells.

Note To highlight a large list in Excel, you can just click in it and press Ctrl+*. Another way is to highlight the top row of the list and then press Ctrl+Shift+Down Arrow. Lists often contain blank rows. If you have a blank row in this list, you have to press Ctrl+Shift+Down Arrow *again* when your highlight reaches the blank row (or rows).

3. Press F5.

4. In the Go To dialog that appears, click Special (see Figure 3-1).

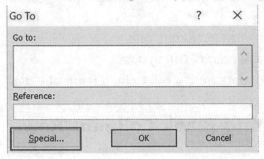

Figure 3-1

5. In the Go To Special dialog that appears, select Blanks (see Figure 3-2). All the blanks in the list are now highlighted.

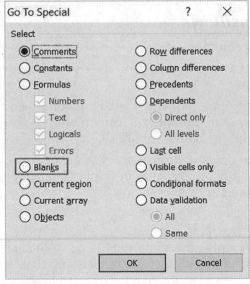

Figure 3-2

6. Type 0 and press Ctrl+Enter to fill in each of the blanks with a 0. Hey presto! All the blank cells now contain 0. Sigh, I love that.

Quickly Entering Formulas Multiple Times

1. Open the file 03_Multiple_entry. In this file, what you want to do is multiply the quantity for each day by the daily rates (B3:B6) so that you end up with an amount for each day.

2. Highlight the range D3:D6.

3. While holding down the Ctrl key, highlight the following ranges: F3:F6, H3:H6, J3:J6, L3:L6, N3:N6, and P3:P6. The areas you have selected change colour.

4. When cell P3 is white, release the Ctrl key.

> **Note** Don't click on anything else, or the highlighted areas lose their highlighting.

5. In cell P3, type =.

6. Click in B3 and press F4 until the cell contains $B3. (You do this to fix the column in this cell so that all formulas using it refer to column B but row 3 has no dollar sign as you want its number to change as it is copied to other rows to prevent the cell from moving when you copy it into all the other cells.)

7. In cell P3, type *.

8. Click on cell O3.

9. Press Ctrl+Enter. The formula now appears in all the areas you highlighted in step 3.

You can see the final numbers in the sheet called Multiple Entry Solution in the file 03_Multiple_entry.

> **Note** If you are using a formula, ensure that it references the cells appropriate for the last entry—the one that appears in white.

Repeating Headings

You can use this variation of the technique just shown to quickly enter headings that are missing. After I learnt this technique from Bill Jelen (MrExcel), people asked me for help with it twice in the next hour. This handy trick saved one woman I know over an hour of tedious work every week!

> **Note** Alas, this technique doesn't work on pivot tables, but the good news is that there is a Repeating Item function in Excel 2010 (and later) pivot tables that does exactly the same thing.

Let's say that in the file 03_Repeating_headings, you see the following entries, starting at cell A1:

Jacket	Purple	12
	Black	25
Trousers	Green	100
	Check	70

You want the entries Jacket and Trousers to repeat so that you end up with this:

Jacket	Purple	12
Jacket	Black	25
Trousers	Green	100
Trousers	Check	70

1. Highlight A1:A4 (i.e., the column with Jacket and Trousers), which contains the blanks you need to fix.

2. Press F5.

3. In the Go To dialog that appears, click Special.

4. In the Go To Special dialog that appears, click Blanks. All the blanks in the list are now selected.

5. Type =, click in cell A1, and press Ctrl+Enter. Excel fills in each of the blanks by repeating the headings as appropriate. Yeah, baby!

Cleaning, Combining, and Amending Existing Data

Sometimes in Excel you get the virtual equivalent of dust—trailing spaces that you can't really see that are definitely there. For example, a word may look okay in a worksheet, but when you check it in the formula bar, you notice that the cursor is a few spaces after the end of the word or there are extra spaces at the beginning or in the middle. The problem with such dust is that it can throw off formulas that reference the dusty data because Excel will not find a match if two instances are not exactly the same.

In this section you will also see how to find and replace data when you need to quickly update data, as well as how to combine multiple cells together into one cell (in a process called *concatenating*). You will also find out how to quickly copy existing formatting onto other cells by using the Format Painter. You are also going to have a look at what to do when Excel thinks you have made a mistake and how you can use a formula to extract specific pieces of data. Finally, you are going to see how to use the Iferror() function to substitute an entry of your choice for an error message.

Using the Trim() Function to Clean and Replace "Dusty" Data

To clean up extra unwanted spaces, you can use the Trim() function. Generally speaking, you should assume that you can use this function on only one column at a time.

1. Open the file 03_Trim and notice that the Payee column has some extra spaces in some of the names (see cells B4 and B5).

> **Note** You may have to click the yellow button at the top that says Enable Content.

2. In cell I2, type =Trim (and click in cell B2 (i.e., the first cell of the column you want to clean up). Then press Enter

3. Copy this formula down to cell I925.

4. Highlight your corrected entries and select Home | Copy (or click Ctrl+C).

5. Click at the top of the column that contains the entries with spaces (i.e., cell B2).

6. Select Home | Paste | Paste Values (see Figure 3-3).

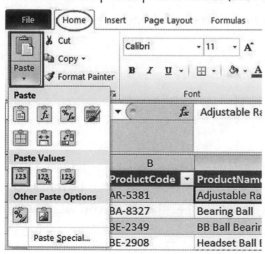

Figure 3-3

7. In the Paste Special dialog that appears, select Values Only to ensure that only values are entered in this cell.

8. Click on Values Only. The payee names are now corrected (with no extra spaces).

> **Note** You can also nest the Trim() function within another function. For example, if you are using a Vlookup() function, instead of using this:
>
> `=Vlookup()(cell, array, , )`
>
> you could use this:
>
> `=Vlookup()(Trim(cell), array, , )`
>
> You can read more about the Vlookup() function in Chapter 4, "The Vlookup() Function: An Excel Essential."

Using Find and Replace

Another approach that has been suggested to me in class—and I can see its uses in certain situations—is to use Find and Replace to remove extra spaces. However, the problem with this tactic is that it often removes the space between names, whereas Trim() is clever enough not to do that.

However, if you need to update numbers (e.g., to update years for training files), Find and Replace works perfectly. For example, to change the year 2009 to 2016 in all cases, you would use the following steps:

1. Open the file 03_Find_and_replace.

2. Highlight the Date column and select Home | Find & Select (see Figure 3-4).

Figure 3-4

3. In the Find and Replace dialog that appears, select the Replace tab.

4. In the Find What box, type 2009 (i.e., what you want to be replaced).

5. In the Replace With box, type 2016 (i.e., the value you want used). See Figure 3-5.

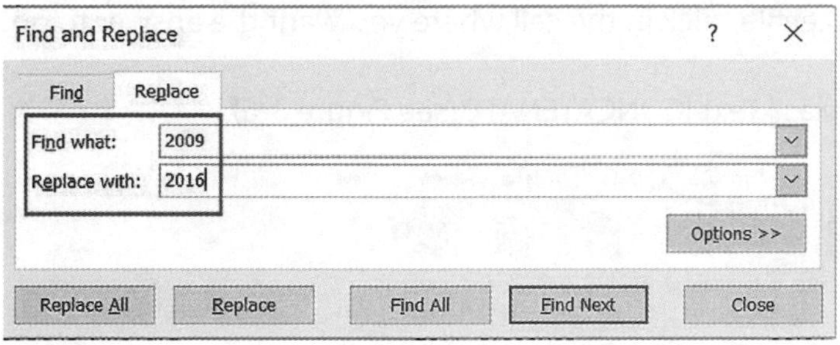

Figure 3-5

6. Click Replace All to do all the replacements in one go or click Replace as many times as needed to replace them individually. (If you choose to click Replace, your cursor should be positioned at the top of the column that contains the data you want to replace.)

Concatenating: Combining Multiple Cells into One Cell

Concatenation involves combining the contents of two or more cells together. Alas, it's not half as exciting as it sounds. But it's very useful for combining the contents of two or more cells together. Here you are going to learn about two methods. The first one involves using a formula. The second one involves using the Concatenate() function.

Concatenating Using a Formula

The following steps assume that you want to combine the first name Ebenezer in cell B2 and the surname Scrooge in C2 into one cell, so you end up with Ebenezer Scrooge in cell D2.

1. In a blank Excel file, click in the cell where you want the answer to go: D2.

2. Type =B2&" "&C2 and press Enter. Cell D2 now contains the text Ebenezer Scrooge.

> **Note** If you use just =B2&C2 instead of =B2&" "&C2, you end up with EbenezerScrooge in cell D2. Remember that Excel sees a space as a character, and you have to treat it as such. Therefore, if you want to include a space between the contents of the two cells you're concatenating, be sure to include the " " between them.

Using the Concatenate() Text Function

The following steps show another way to combine the first name Ebenezer in cell B2 and the surname Scrooge in C2 into one cell, but this time you end up with Ebenezer Scrooge in cell E2.

1. In a blank Excel file, click in the cell where you want the answer to go: E2.

2. Select Formulas | Text |CONCATENATE (see Figure 3-6).

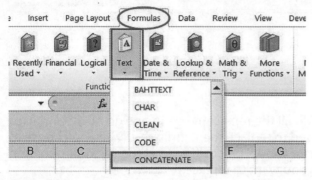

Figure 3-6

3. In the Function Arguments dialog that appears (see Figure 3-7), click in the Text1 box and then click in cell B2.

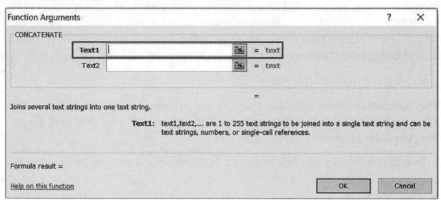

Figure 3-7

4. Click in the Text2 box and then enter "   " (for the space).

5. Click in the Text3 box and then click in cell C2.

6. Click OK when you are finished. Cell E2 now contains the text Ebenezer Scrooge.

> **Note** If you want to use these entries as values, you have to se-
> lect Home | Copy | Paste Special | Paste Values. If you just try to
> copy the text from E2 into another cell (e.g., G2), you see only
> a blank and not Ebenezer Scrooge because Excel has adjusted
> the formula so that it will now be attempting to concatenate E2
> and F2.

Using the Format Painter to Copy Existing Formatting to Other Cells

It is likely that at some point you will inherit a spreadsheet from someone else and find that it already has some sort of formatting on it. The easiest way to maintain the existing formatting in anything you add to the spreadsheet is to use the Format Painter option, which essentially copies formatting from one cell to another. You can use it for number formats and also for copying conditional formatting.

> **Note** You can't use the Format Painter to move formatting from one file to another. Instead, though, you can copy and paste the cells with the desired formatting into another workbook and then use your Format Painter to apply that formatting to the rest of the file.

> **Survival Tip** Format Painter works in Microsoft Word as well.

1. Open the file 03_Format_painter. In this case, you want to copy the formatting from the numbers in the Desired Format column to the numbers in the Copy Format column.

2. Click on the cell with the desired formatting: B2

3. Select Home | Format Painter (see Figure 3-8). A small brush appears on your mouse pointer.

Figure 3-8

4. Highlight the entire Copy Format column to apply the desired formatting to these cells. Presto: Formatting copied!

> **Note** You can double-click the Format Painter icon to continue copying this format to other cells. Press Esc when you're done doing this.

Adding Leading Zeros to (and Keeping Them with) Numbers

Depending on where in the world you are, you may need to enter numbers with leading zeros. For example, in Ireland a telephone number begins with a zero. In the United States, some zip codes start with 0. With entries such as these, you do not want Excel to strip the leading zero and return something like 99555111 (instead of the Irish phone number 099555111) or 1982 (instead of the U.S. zip code 01982). There are two ways to get around this:

- You can enter the number as follows: `099-555-111`. Excel retains the leading zero because the hyphens help Excel recognize this entry as text.

- You can enter an `'` (apostrophe) before you enter the rest of the number (i.e., `'099555111`) to convert the entry to text.

What to Do When Excel Thinks You Have Made an Error

You may at some point see a little green error flag at the top-left side of a cell. (You can see an example of this in the file called 03_Excel_error, in the range D2:D27.) This flag means that Excel thinks you may have made an error. You can remove this flag by highlighting the column that contains the numbers and then clicking the small yellow diamond icon shown in Figure 3-9.

A	B	C	D	E	F
Date	Adults	Children	Total		
02/01/2009	154	◆ ▾ 0	242		
02/01/2009	107		Formula Omits Adjacent Cells		
02/01/2009	85				
03/01/2009	179		Update Formula to Include Cells		
03/01/2009	118		Help on this error		
03/01/2009	164		Ignore Error		
04/01/2009	108		Edit in Formula Bar		
04/01/2009	130		Error Checking Options...		
04/01/2009	154	80	234		

Figure 3-9

The first option on this menu tells you what Excel thinks the error is. (In Figure 3-9, Excel is asking why you haven't included the date values in the Date column in your Sum() formula. This occurs because Excel reads dates as numbers.) The options on this menu vary depending on what Excel thinks the error is. It's usually a good idea just to have a look at this. However, if you are sure that your formula is correct, you can remove the error flag by highlighting the entire column and selecting Ignore Error from the menu.

Extracting Specific Pieces of Data from a Cell to Refine a Data Set

Sometimes you want to extract a piece of data from a list—for example, if you receive an external file (e.g., from a supplier) and want just one bit of the code from that file to match with your records. For example, say that your supplier sends you a product code BMR-000-932, but the bit you need is just the 932 part. In this case, you can use a text function to extract what you need.

There are a number of text functions for extracting specific bits of data from various positions in data. As you read the following sections, use the file 03_Text_functions to see examples of all these functions.

Using Left() to Extract Just the Bit on the Left

Say that you want to extract BMR or BMR- from BMR-000-932, which in the file 03_Text_functions is in cell A3.

1. Click in the column you want your revised data to go into (in this case, cell F3), type =left (, and click in the cell where you want to get the data—in this case A3.

2. Type , 3 to indicate that you want to extract three characters.

3. Press Enter and copy down the formula to cell F19. BMR now appears in all these cells.

4. As you have done previously when you have concatenated cells, the next step is to copy and paste the values, so highlight cells F3:F19 and select Home | Copy. (This time you are going to copy and paste within the same cells.) Note that "marching ants" now appear around this range.

5. Select Home | Paste | Paste Values. You have now replaced the Left() function formula with the first three characters of the entries in column A.

Using Right() to Extract Just the Bit on the Right

Say that you want to extract 932 or -932 from BMR-000-932.

1. Click in the column you want your revised data to go into (in this case, cell G3), type =right (, and click in the cell where you want to get the data—in this case A3.

2. Type , 3 to indicate that you want to extract three characters.

3. Press Enter and copy down the formula to cell G19. 932 now appears in G3.

4. As you have done previously when you have concatenated cells, the next step is to copy and paste the values, so highlight cells G3:G19 and select Home | Copy. (This time you are going to copy and paste within the same cells.) Note that "marching ants" now appear around this range.

5. Select Home | Paste | Paste Values. You have now replaced the Right() function formula with the last three characters of the entries in column A.

Using Mid() to Extract Just the Bit in the Middle

Sometimes you might just want the text from the middle of some data. For example, let's say you want to extract the middle three characters (i.e., the 000) from the value BMR-000-932, which is in cell A3, and then copy the formula down. This function is a little different from the ones you've just seen. It looks like this:

```
=Mid(Input, Start_position, Nbr_of_characters)
```

where:

- Input signifies the string from which to extract a substring.
- Start_position signifies the numeric position in Input_string from which to begin the extraction.
- Nbr_of_characters indicates the number of characters to extract.

1. Click in the column you want your revised data to go into (in this case, cell H3), type =mid(, and click in the cell where you want to get the data—in this case A3.

2. Type , 5 to indicate that the extraction should start five characters from the left.

3. Type , 3 to extract three characters.

4. Press Enter and copy down the formula to cell H19. 000 now appears in H3.

5. As you have done previously when you have concatenated cells, the next step is to copy and paste the values, so highlight cells H3:H19 and select Home | Copy. (This time you are going to copy and paste within the same cells.) Note that "marching ants" now appear around this range.

6. Select Home | Paste | Paste Values. You have now replaced the Mid() function formula with the middle three characters from the entries in column A.

Getting to Know the Wonderful Text() Function

One of my favourite unsung functions is the Text() function. You can use it to easily extract days (the day number and the actual day name), months, or years from a date. It gives you a text answer, which means that while the Text() function is suitable for display, it doesn't work if you need to do calculations with the results. Here is the syntax of this function:

```
Text(Value, Format_text)
```

where:

- Value is a numeric value, a formula that evaluates to a numeric value, or a reference to a cell containing a numeric value.
- Format_text is a numeric formatted as a text string enclosed in quotation marks (e.g., "m/d/yyyy" or "#,##0.00").

Showing the Name of the Day

1. Open a blank file in Excel and type 29 October 2015 (or whatever format you normally use to enter dates) into cell A1.

2. Click in B2, where you want the answer to go, and type =Tex.

3. In the list of functions that appears, double-click Text. =Text (now appears in B2.

4. Click in A1 and type , dddd and then press Enter. You now see Thursday in cell B2.

Showing the Full Name of the Month

1. In the same file you were just using, click in cell C2, where you want the answer to go, and type =Tex.

2. In the list of functions that appears, double-click Text. =Text (now appears in B2.

3. Click in A1 and type , mmmm and then press Enter. You now see October in cell C2.

> **Note** I have just shown you two specific entries, but if you go to Excel Help and search for Text function, you will find lots more information.

Extracting Specific Pieces of Date Entries

Sometimes you need to extract just specific pieces of a date from an entry. As you read the following sections, use the file 03_Date_extraction to see examples of all these functions.

Extracting the Day

The Day() function extracts the day part from a date. So, for example, given the date 29 October 2015, the Day() function returns 29.

1. Open a blank file in Excel and type in 29 October 2015 (in whatever format you normally enter your dates) into cell A1.

2. Click in B2, where you want the answer to go, and type =Day.

3. In the list of functions that appears, double-click Day, and =Day(now appears in B2.

4. Click in A1 and press Enter. You now see the day number 29 in B2.

Extracting the Month

The Month() function extracts the month number part from a date. So, for example, given the date 29 October 2015 in A1, the Month() function returns 10.

1. Click in C1 and type =Month.

2. In the list of functions that appears, double-click Month, and =Month(now appears in the cell.

3. Click in cell A1. Type) and press Enter. You now see the month number 10 in C1.

Extracting the Year

The Year() function extracts the year number part from a date. So, for example, given the date 29 October 2015 in A1, the Year() function returns 2015.

1. Click in D1 and type =Year.

2. In the list of functions that appears, double-click Year, and =Year(now appears in the cell.

3. Click in cell A1.

4. Press Enter. You now see the year 2015 in D1.

Extracting the Week Number

The Weeknum() function shows you the number of the week in which a date falls. Excel assumes that the week begins on Sunday. If you also assume that the week begins on Sunday, follow these steps to use Weeknum() with the date 29 October 2015 in A1.

1. In cell E2, enter =Weeknum(.

2. Click in A1 and press Enter. Excel gives you the answer 44, indicating that 29 October 2015 fell in week 44 of the year.

However, if you don't agree with Excel about the week beginning on Sunday, you need to add a second part to the function. For example, if your week begins on Monday, you follow these steps:

1. In cell E2, enter `=Weeknum(a2,2)`.

2. Click in A1 and press Enter. Excel gives you the answer 44, indicating that 29 October 2015 fell in week 44 of the year.

> **Note** For a complete list of the numbers to use with this function, depending on the day you use as the beginning of the week, see the Excel help for the Weeknum() function.

> **Survival Tip** Sometimes when you use the date functions described above, instead of getting numbers, you get actual dates. If this happens to you, you need to highlight the column and convert it to General by selecting Home | General (see Figure 3-10).

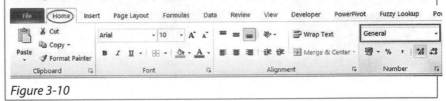

Figure 3-10

Further Techniques for Extracting Specific Pieces of Data from a Cell

Quite often when you're preparing data for a pivot table, you need only specific pieces of data. For example, say that you want to analyse only the transactions that are over a certain amount. The way you usually do this is by using an If() function. The following sections describe how to handle three common real-life scenarios. (There are many other scenarios we could look at, but these three should be enough to get you going.)

Scenario 1: Include Only Items That Meet a Certain Condition

Say that you only want to include items that meet a certain condition in your data set, such as transactions in the Publications category. (You could also do this by using a filter, but there may be times when you need to clearly identify the data rather than use a filter.) To find these items, you can add a column to identify whether a category in your list is a publication. You want to see Yes appear for items that are in the Publications category and No otherwise.

1. Open the file 03_Data_cleanup_only_specific_categories.

2. Click on the Transactions sheet and note the word Publications is already in cell I1.

3. Click in F1, type `Publications?`, and note that the table automatically expands to include the new column.

4. Click in cell F2 and select Formulas | Logical | IF (see Figure 3-11).

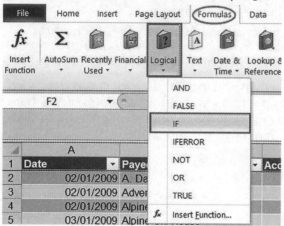

Figure 3-11

5. In the Function Arguments dialog box that appears (see Figure 3-12), click in the Logical_test box, click in cell D2, and type `[@Category]=$I$1` (pressing F4 to fix add the dollar signs as you type I1).

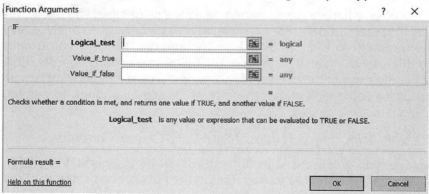

Figure 3-12

6. In the Value_if_true box, type `"Yes"`.

7. In the Value_if_false box, type `"No"`. You can see the completed formula by double-clicking on cell F2 (see Figure 3-13).

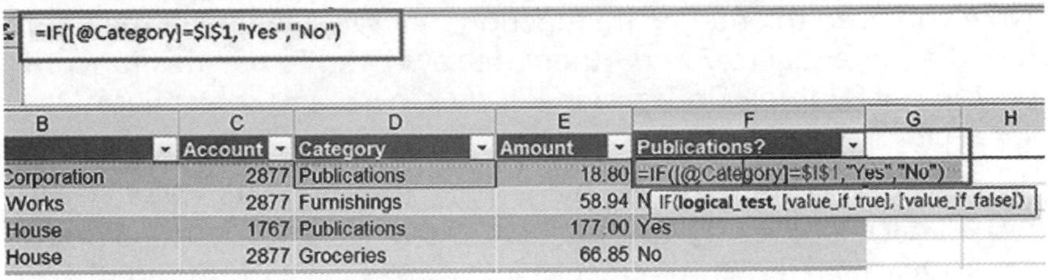

	B	C	D	E	F	G	H
		▼ Account ▼	Category	▼ Amount	▼	Publications? ▼	
	Corporation	2877	Publications		18.80	=IF(([@Category]=$I$1,"Yes","No")	
	Works	2877	Furnishings		58.94	N IF(**logical_test**, [value_if_true], [value_if_false])	
	House	1767	Publications		177.00	Yes	
	House	2877	Groceries		66.85	No	

Top formula bar: `=IF([@Category]=$I$1,"Yes","No")`

Figure 3-13

Survival Tip If you use text entries in a formula, you must use quotation marks when you type those entries in the Value_if_true and Value_if_false boxes in the Function Arguments dialog box. The formula will return Name! if you omit them. As I often say in class, "You don't have to use them, but it won't work if you don't."

Note In this example, why did I ask you to put Publications into a separate cell (I1)? In the future, if you want to do a different analysis on another category, like Vacation, all you have to do is replace Publications in cell I1 with Vacation to get the new result.

Scenario 2: Identifying Only Entries That Have a Gap of a Certain Size

Now say that you want to identify only those entries where the gap between two dates exceeds a certain number.

1. Open the file 03_Date_difference_if_function.

2. Click the Sales Data sheet, in which you want to identify all the transactions where the difference between Ship Date and Order Date was greater than or equal to 7.

3. In cell Q1, type 7.

4. In cell Q2, type the heading Ship Minus Order Days (and again notice how the table expands to automatically include this new heading).

5. In the Ship Minus Order Days column, you need to enter a formula that subtracts OrderDate from ShipDate to show the number of days of difference. To enter this formula, click in cell Q3, type =, click in P3, enter −, and click in O3. Note that what appears in cell Q3 is = [@Ship-Date]-[@OrderDate].

Survival Tip Excel sees dates as numbers that began at a specific date. Therefore, it sees the date for today as being bigger than the date for yesterday.

6. Press Enter to copy down the whole formula.

7. Now you need to enter an If() function that says On time if the figure is less than or equal to 7 and otherwise says Late. To use this function, type 7 in cell Q1, type On Time? in R2, click in R3, and select Formulas | Logical | IF.

8. In the Function Arguments dialog box that appears (refer to Figure 3-8), click in the Logical_test box, click in cell Q3, and note that what appears is `[@[Ship minus Order days]]`. Beside it type `<=$Q$1`. When it's complete, it should read `[@[Ship minus Order days]]<=$Q$1`.

9. In the Value_if_true box, type `"On Time"`.

10. In the Value_if_false box, type `"Late"`.

11. Press Enter to copy down the whole formula. You can see the completed formula by double-clicking on cell R3 in the worksheet called Completed (see Figure 3-14).

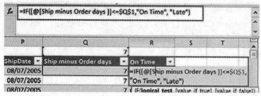

Figure 3-14

Scenario 3: Using Either a Condition or the Original Entry

Now say that you want to group together all the entries that meet a certain criterion, and for anything that doesn't meet the condition, you want the original entry to be used. In this scenario, if a product begins with the word Mountain, you want to see the phrase Mountain bike; otherwise, you want the actual entry to be used. In this case, you will be using a function you have already come across, Left(), to identify the first eight letters as Mountain.

1. Open the file 03_Use_when_if_function.

2. Open the sheet Sales Data. Note that Mountain has already been entered in cell D1.

3. In B2, type `Mountain Bike?`.

4. Click in cell B3 and select Formulas | Logical | IF.

5. In the Function Arguments dialog box that appears (refer to Figure 3-12), click in the Logical_test box, enter `Left (`, click in cell A3, and note that that `[@[Product name ]]` now appears. Beside it type `,8)=$D$1`. When it's complete, it should read `Left([@[Product`

name]],8)=$D$1. (Basically this formula asks whether the first eight characters in this cell are equal to Mountain.)

6. In the Value_if_true box, type $D$1.

7. In the Value_if_false box, click on A3 and note that [@[Product name]] appears.

8. Press Enter to copy down the whole formula. You can see the completed formula by double-clicking on cell B3 in the worksheet called Completed (see Figure 3-15).

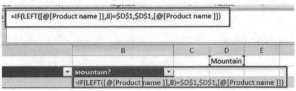

=IF(LEFT([@[Product name]],8)=$D$1,$D$1,[@[Product name]])

	B	C	D	E
			Mountain	
	Mountain?			
	=IF(LEFT([@[Product name]],8)=$D$1,$D$1,[@[Product name]])			

Figure 3-15

Identifying and Removing Duplicates

Another key part of cleaning up data, particularly when you will be using Vlookup(), is identifying and removing duplicates.

Using Conditional Formatting to Identify Duplicates

Say that you want to use colour to identify entries that have been duplicated (which in Excel terms means they were entered twice or more). You can use conditional formatting to identify these duplicates.

1. Open the file 03_Duplicate_entries.

2. Click in cell A2 and press Ctrl+Shift+Down Arrow.

3. Select Home | Conditional Formatting | Highlight Cells Rules | Duplicate Values (see Figure 3-16).

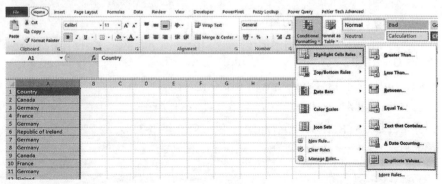

Figure 3-16

4. In the Duplicate Values dialog that appears, accept the defaults by clicking OK (see Figure 3-17). All the duplicated values are now coloured red.

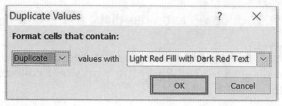

Figure 3-17

Removing Conditional Formatting

1. Still in 03_Duplicate_entries, click in cell A2 and press Ctrl+Shift+Down Arrow.

2. Select Home | Conditional Formatting | Clear Rules | Clear Rules from Selected Cells (see Figure 3-18). Excel removes the conditional formatting.

Figure 3-18

Removing Duplicate Entries

Once you have identified those tricky little duplicates, how do you remove them? It's actually very straightforward.

1. Open the file 03_Duplicate_entries_remove.

2. Click in cell A2 and press Ctrl+Shift+Down Arrow.

3. Select Data | Remove Duplicates (see Figure 3-19).

Figure 3-19

4. In the Remove Duplicates dialog that appears (see Figure 3-20), click OK. Excel removes the duplicates and tells you how many records it has removed and how many unique records are left.

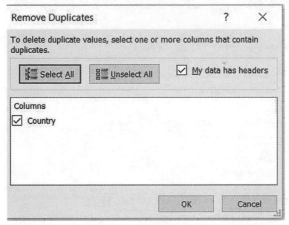

Figure 3-20

Using the Iferror() Function

Sometimes you don't want the user to have to see a particular error message. One of the most useful new functions in Excel 2007 and later is Iferror(). Essentially, you use this function to tell Excel what error message to give instead of its usual error messages, like #N/A, #VALUE!, #REF!, #DIV/0!, #NUM!, #NAME?, and #NULL!. I think of it as a comforting function you can wrap around an error message to instead give the user a kinder, gentler error message.

For example, if someone has entered a date incorrectly, by default, Excel spits out the #VALUE! error instead of returning the correct year. But you can amend the formula in this case so Excel instead returns an error message such as incorrect date or just 0. Here's the syntax for this function:

```
Iferror(Value, Value_if_error)
```

where:

• *Value* is the formula or cell entry that might return an error message.

• *Value_if_error* is what you want to appear instead of the default error message.

1. Open the file 03_If_error. In cell E3, the Year() function has been entered, but because the date 31/2/2015 doesn't exist, Year() returns a #VALUE! message.

2. In cell F3, type =Iferror(Year(D3),"Check the date") to return the more friendly message Check the date (see Figure 3-21). Press Enter.

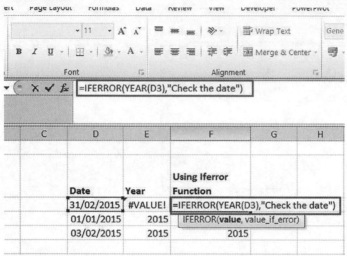

Figure 3-21

> **Note** If you want a blank to appear instead of a message, enter " " for *Value_if_error* (e.g., Iferror(Year(D3)," ")).

Summary

This chapter has looked at further clean-up you can do with data. If you work with Excel a lot, a fair chunk of your work revolves around data cleaning. However, now that you've read this chapter, you have some Excel techniques for doing this cleaning quickly rather than (pause for shudder) manually.

Chapter 4 The Vlookup() Function: An Excel Essential

Here's a question I often get asked in class: "I've got matching data in two locations that I have to use together. Why can't I just copy and paste any new data when it changes?"

Does your data change? I suspect the answer is "er, yes." In that case, you *could* copy and paste, but it's much smarter to use the Vlookup() function to capture the changes.

If you use Copy and Paste to insert data instead of using Vlookup(), you will have to manually update your spreadsheet. That means locating the place where the data changed, copying the data, and then pasting it in to your own spreadsheet.

This isn't a robust method of updating a spreadsheet. For example, what happens if you forget what data you have copied and pasted into your spreadsheet? And what happens if the new data isn't in the same order as it was before? Yep, speaking from experience here, that's when you will have officially made a dog's dinner of your data, and *that is not a good thing*.

It's worth learning how to use Vlookup() because with this function, your data is automatically updated, so it's always accurate and safe.

Essentially, the Vlookup() function allows you to match up the same data from two different data sources. It is used for many Excel scenarios, and knowing how to use it properly will save you time and grlef.

Your data sources could be on the same worksheet, in separate worksheets in the same workbook, or—as is often the case—in different workbooks. We will look at each of these situations in this chapter.

In terms of your Excel survival, the Vlookup() function is like your water bottle. It's a lifesaver. However, it does have a few idiosyncrasies you need to be aware of.

Understanding the Vlookup() Function Syntax

Here's the syntax of the Vlookup() function (which you can find yourself by selecting Formulas | Lookup & Reference | VLOOKUP; see Figure 4-1):

```
Vlookup(Lookup_value,Table_array,
        Col_index_num,Range_lookup)
```

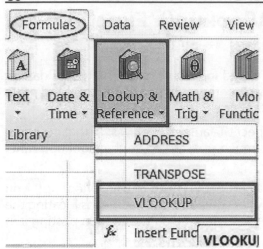

Figure 4-1

Okay, don't panic. Let's just walk through it.

I want you to imagine a scenario that will make it easier to understand the structure above: You are buying a bottle of water in your favourite supermarket. It will be scanned through the till system using the barcode. Next, the till will check this barcode against the supermarket's master list of products so it can update the stock list and charge you the correct amount for the water. This all happens so that your receipt will show the correct description and price for your bottle of water.

Here's what happens: The till checks the barcode on the bottle (that's the *Lookup_value*) and compares it to the master list of products. For this to work, the barcode has to be in two places (i.e., on the bottle and in the supermarket's master list of products).

The till system goes to the supermarket master list of products (*Table_array*) and gets the number of the column in that list that holds the description (*Col_index_num*) of the product. It then goes through the same process again to get the price. This is how the correct description and price for your water get onto your receipt.

The till system is then told that if it wants an exact match between the barcode on the bottle and the barcode in the supermarket database, it needs to refer to *Range_lookup*.

> **Note** Setting *Range_lookup* to FALSE ensures that the two data sources get an exact match. You can also leave *Range_lookup* blank in scenarios where you don't want an exact match. A good example of this is when you want to match an exam mark to an exam grade. Let's say Joe Bloggs gets an exam mark of

92%. His grade is assigned based on the fact that his mark falls into the 90%–100% range. When this happens, Joe is assigned an A for the exam. To set up a Vlookup() function for this, you would make sure that anyone who gets an exam mark between 90% and 100% gets an A. Unlike in the barcode example, here you do not want an exact match between 92% and the A grade result because this would mean that only anyone who gets exactly 92% would get an A grade. Also, it would assume that *Table_array* will always be listed alphabetically. To see how this is done, check out the file 04_Vlookup()_true.

Troubleshooting Vlookup(): Dealing with #N/A Errors

Before getting into the sections that present situations where you use Vlookup(), this section provides some tips on avoiding frustration while using Vlookup(). Of course, functions don't always work smoothly, and here we look at some of the troubles you are most likely to meet.

Anyone who has ever done a Vlookup() has experienced #N/A errors. What can you do to keep the number of these problems to a minimum? I usually suggest thinking of these three *L*s:

- To the *left*
- *Like*
- On the same *line*

Here's what I mean by this: The *Lookup_value* has to be to the *left* of your formula, identical to (*like*) the first column of the table, and on the same row (or *line*). And here are even more details:

- To the *left* means the lookup value needs to be to the left of your formula (or, if you imagine a clock, think of the 6:00 to 12:00 portion of the face), on the same line. Note in the Situation 1 example later in this chapter that the SalesTerritoryKey is to the left of the Vlookup() formula that begins in cell I2.

- *Like* means the lookup value should be identical to the first column of the *Table_array*. Note that the matching column (i.e., the value in *Lookup_value*) has to be the first column of the table (or, as I like to joke in class, it doesn't have to be, but it doesn't work otherwise!).

  This means your data types must be the same. For example, if your lookup value is a number, and Excel is reading it as text, prepare to see many many #N/As because the Vlookup() function thinks they have nothing in common and refuses to work. You can check that your number is not text by clicking on the cell you want to check.

Next, select the Home tab and ensure that the Number group says General or Number and not Text. If it says Text, and the matching value in your *Table_array* is a number, the Vlookup() will not work. If data is text, this is indicated by the green marker in the top-left corner of the cell. If you click it, you get the option Convert to Number or Convert to Text, which you can use to convert your data so that the data types of both the *Lookup_value* and the first column of the *Table_array* are the same.

In addition, the entries in the first column of the table array have to be unique. This may sometimes require the creation of a helper cell (which is covered later in this chapter).

• On the same *line* really means "on the same row," but to make this little memory aid, I wanted a third *L* here.

If any of these conditions are not met—particularly either of the first two—you will probably have trouble with your Vlookup().

Understanding When to Use Vlookup()

The following sections describe a few situations when you should use Vlookup():

• Situation 1: Matching up data in the same worksheet and file
• Situation 2: Matching up data in the same file but different worksheets
• Situation 3: Matching up data with a formula and table array in two different files

Obviously, these are not the only ones, but they are very typical ones.

Situation 1: Matching Up Data in the Same Worksheet and File

In this section, you'll see how to use Vlookup() to match up data in the same worksheet. The files you need for this section are in the Working Files folder. In this example, you will pull in SalesTerritoryCountry starting at cell I2 for the SalesTerritoryKey. Your matching list will be coming from A1:E12 on the same worksheet.

1. Open the file 04_Vlookup_same_worksheet.
2. Click the Sales Territories sheet.
3. Click in I2 and select Formulas | Lookup | Reference | VLOOKUP.
4. In the Function Arguments dialog that appears (see Figure 4-2), click in the Lookup_value box and click in H2.

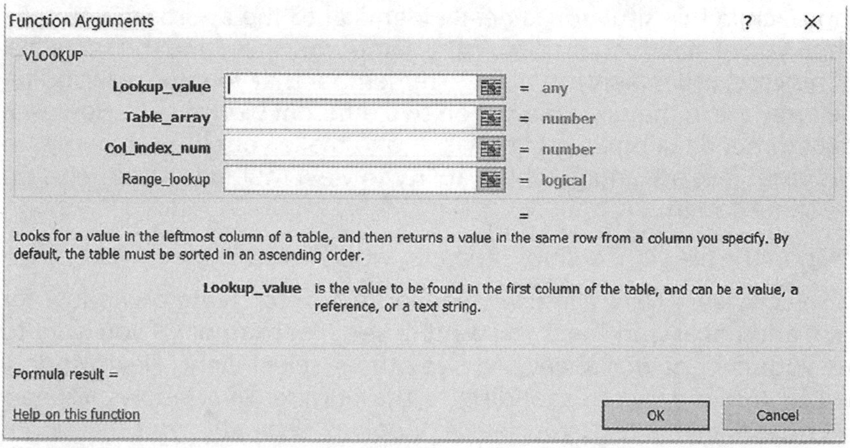

Function Arguments		?	×

VLOOKUP

Lookup_value			🔢	= any
Table_array			🔢	= number
Col_index_num			🔢	= number
Range_lookup			🔢	= logical

=

Looks for a value in the leftmost column of a table, and then returns a value in the same row from a column you specify. By default, the table must be sorted in an ascending order.

           Lookup_value is the value to be found in the first column of the table, and can be a value, a reference, or a text string.

Formula result =

Help on this function   [OK]   [Cancel]

Figure 4-2

5. Click in the Table_array box, highlight the part of the spreadsheet that contains the data (A1:E12), and fix the range by pressing F4 to apply dollar signs to it. You now see $A$1 : $E$12 in the Table_array box.

> **Note** It is very important that you fix the range by pressing F4. If you don't, the range will change as you copy down the formula, so it will start reading A2:E13 as you copy it down.

6. Click in the Col_index_num box and type 4 (because SalesTerritory-Country—the data you want to pull in—is the fourth column from the left in the *Table_array* part of the formula).

7. In the Range_lookup box, type False. This means you want an exact match, regardless of how the first column of the *Table_array* bit is sorted. Excel tends to assume that the first column of the *Table_array* list will be sorted alphabetically, but that is not always what you want.

8. Click OK, and you should see United States in cell I2.

9. Press Enter to copy down the whole formula.

10. Test the formula by changing D10 (sales territory 9) from Australia to Ireland. You now see this change reflected in cell I10. In cell I10, you now see Ireland. Change it back to Australia. As you can see, any changes in the *Table_array* portion are reflected in the answers to the formula. So the changes happen automatically.

Situation 2: Matching Up Data in the Same File but Different Worksheets

Sometimes you need to match up data when a formula is stored in one worksheet and a table array is stored in a different worksheet. The approach in this situation is nearly identical to the approach you take when you're matching up data in the same worksheet and the same file. In this case, you mainly just need to remember that your formula and table array are in the same file but on two different worksheets. However, I recommend taking an additional step to make your life a lot easier in this case: Take advantage of the ability to view multiple worksheets on the same screen.

1. Open the file 04_Vlookup_separate_worksheets.

2. Select View | New Window (see Figure 4-3) to create a window for each additional worksheet you want to see. (For example, if you want to see your current worksheet and two others, select View | New Window twice.) A number corresponding to the number of windows appears after the filename (e.g., you see 04_Vlookup_separate_worksheets: 3 if you have three windows).

Figure 4-3

3. Select View | Arrange All.

4. In the Arrange dialog that appears, check Windows of Active Workbook to view all the worksheets on the same screen and leave Tiled selected (see Figure 4-4). You can now view two files side by side.

Figure 4-4

Closing Extra Windows

If you find that you have been a little too enthusiastic in clicking New Window, and it looks as though windows have started to reproduce, you need to close some windows.

1. Click in the window you want to close and then click the X at the top-right of the window to close it.

2. Repeat until you have open only the windows that you require.

3. Select View | Arrange All.

4. In the Arrange dialog that appears, leave Tiled selected.

5. Click the sheets you want to view— Sales Territories and Enter Formula on This Sheet—so you can see them at the same time. Sales Territories should be visible on one side, and Enter Formula on This Sheet should be visible on the other, as shown in Figure 4-5.

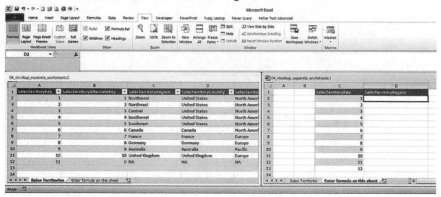

Figure 4-5

6. In the sheet called Enter Formula on This Sheet, click in D2 and select Formulas | Lookup & Reference | VLOOKUP.

7. Click in cell C2 in the same worksheet.

8. Click in the Table_array box in the Function Arguments dialog, highlight the worksheet (Sales Territories) that contains the data from A1:E12, and fix the range by pressing F4 to apply dollar signs to it.

> **Note** It is very important that you fix the range by pressing F4. If you don't, the range will change as you copy down the formula, so it will start reading A2:E13 as you copy it down.

9. Click in the Col_index_num box and type 3 (because SalesTerritoryRegion—the data you want to pull in—is the third column from the left in the *table_array* part of the formula).

10. In the Range_lookup box, type FALSE.

11. Click OK and copy down the formula to D12. You should now see Northwest in D2 and other regions entered in the range D3:D12. (The last entry should be United Kingdom in D12.)

Situation 3: Matching Up Data in Two Different Files

Before you start looking closely at this situation, here are some things to consider:

- Having all the files that relate to a Vlookup() in one folder generally reduces the number of problems with broken links. You can check what files you are using by selecting Data | Edit Links. In the Edit Links dialog that appears, make sure you are in the file that is pulling in the data from the other files (see Figure 4-6).

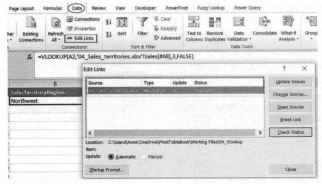

Figure 4-6

- Make sure both files involved in the data matching are open. If they are not and you already have a Vlookup() function created, you may see the REF! message when you open the file that contains the Vlookup() function.

- Make sure you are in the file that is pulling in the data from the other files.

- Sometimes if you get the REF! message, it just means the file needs to be opened. Use an Iferror() function around it to say "please check that the file is open." (You can read more about this function in Chapter 3, "Further Cleaning, Slicing, and Dicing.")

- When you are selecting your table array and it is in another file, dollar signs appear automatically on the range you have selected. Of course, a better idea is to convert your table array to a table, as discussed later in this chapter.

Get ready to rumble—or at least get your files visible—and follow these steps:

1. Open the two files 04_Sales_territories and 04_Vlookup_functions_ files. Ensure that all other spreadsheets are closed.

2. Select View | Arrange All, and in the Arrange dialog that appears, ensure that Windows of Active Workbook is not selected and leave Tiled selected. Your two files should now be open and placed side by side.

3. Click in cell B2 in the 04_Vlookup_functions_files file.

4. Follow the steps in the section "Situation 2: Matching Up Data in the Same File but Different Worksheets" to have your Vlookup() pull in SalesTerritoryRegion. However, this time, when it comes to the table array, highlight the column heads SalesTerritoryKey, SalesTerritoryRegion, SalesTerritoryCountry, and SalesTerritoryGroup in the 04_Sales_territories file and then press Ctrl+Shift+Down Arrow. The filename now comes into the formula. In this version, it is =Vlookup()(A2,'sales territories.xlsx'!Sales[#All],3,FALSE), but in your file, it will probably be different because you will have it stored in a different location.

5. Copy down the formula to B13. You can check your answers in the sheet called Completed.

How to Solve Common Vlookup() Problems

Alas, while the Vlookup() function is immensely useful, it doesn't always work as expected, and in this section I cover some of the most common issues.

Handling Missing Data

The most common reason that you end up with missing data is that your table array has not been extended to include the new data (e.g., a new sales territory) that you have added to the list with the lookup value.

1. Open the file 04_Vlookup_missing_data. If you look in cell I11, you see #N/A.

2. Click on the formula, and you see that the table array is referencing only $A$1:$E$11, although you now have entries in A1:E12.

3. Update your formula to include the new data. You can do this by clicking on the formula in cell I2.

4. Call up the Vlookup() Function Arguments dialog box by clicking the fx button (see Figure 4-7).

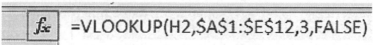

f_x =VLOOKUP(H2,$A$1:$E$12,3,FALSE)

Figure 4-7

5. Edit the *table_array* part of the formula to reflect the new data range: $A$1:$E$13. You can do this either by changing the $E$12 to $E$13 or by reselecting the range to include $A$1:$E$13. To do this, click on the selection box next to Table_array in the Function Arguments dialog, as shown in Figure 4-8, and highlight the range $A$1:$E$13. Click on the selection box again to return to the main Vlookup() dialog box.

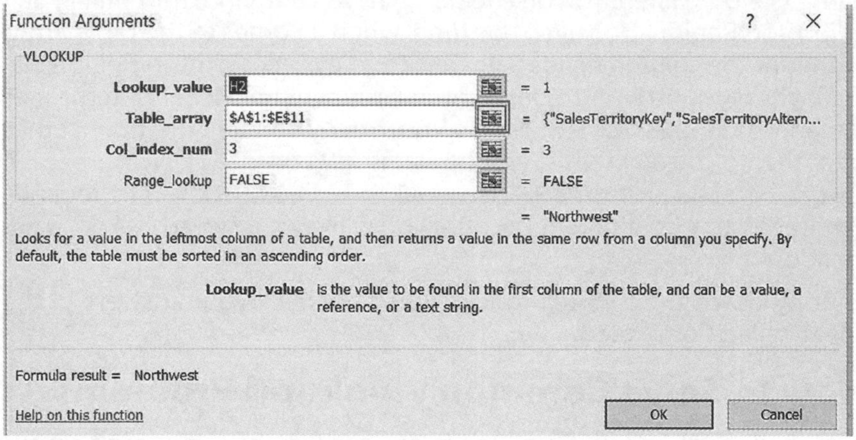

Function Arguments	?	✕

VLOOKUP

Lookup_value	I2		= 1
Table_array	$A$1:$E$11		= {"SalesTerritoryKey","SalesTerritoryAltern...
Col_index_num	3		= 3
Range_lookup	FALSE		= FALSE

= "Northwest"

Looks for a value in the leftmost column of a table, and then returns a value in the same row from a column you specify. By default, the table must be sorted in an ascending order.

Lookup_value   is the value to be found in the first column of the table, and can be a value, a reference, or a text string.

Formula result =   Northwest

Help on this function   OK   Cancel

Figure 4-8

6. Click OK and copy down the formula to cell I12. You should now see Ireland in cell I11.

> **Note** Even though the error showed up in cell I11, you begin the correction in cell I2 because you want to make sure the correction is applied to all the formulas, not just the one it shows up in.

Using the Table Feature to Solve the Missing Data Problem

However, it might be better to just get around this issue and resolve the problem permanently, particularly if the *table_array* part of the formula is regularly getting additions. To do this, you can convert a table array (where you will be pulling your matching data from) into a table. You've already seen tables in Chapter 2, but here's a quick reminder:

1. Open the file 04_Vlookup_missing_data_table.

2. In the Sales Territories sheet, click on cell C8 and press Ctrl+T (or select Insert | Table).

3. In the Create Table dialog box that appears, make sure the My Table Has Headers box is checked and click OK.

4. Click anywhere in the table, click the Design tab, type `Sales` under Table Name, and press Enter to name the table Sales (see Figure 4-9).

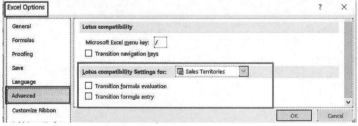

Figure 4-9

5. Click in I2.

6. Follow the steps in the section "Situation 1: Matching Up Data in the Same Worksheet and File" to enter your Vlookup() function. (Note that you see one important difference: Your *table_array* part should now read Sales[#All] instead of A1:E12.)

7. In cell A13:E13, enter the following new territory:

12	12	Hungary	Eastern Europe	Europe

8. In cell H13, type 12.

9. Copy down the formula from I2 to I13. Hungary now appears in cell I13, and you don't have to make any changes to the *table_array* part of the formula.

> **Note** Sometimes using a table makes cell references case-sensitive. I discovered (after checking at Experts Exchange) that you can do the following to fix this issue:
> 1. Choose File | Options.
> 2. In the Excel Options dialog that appears, scroll down the Advanced tab until you see Lotus Compatibility Settings For section and make sure the box Transition Formula Evaluation is unticked. You can see this in Figure 4-10.

Figure 4-10

Handling Different Data Types

If the data types of the lookup value and the first column of a table array are not the same data type, you can end up with many many #N/A errors. This can happen, for example, if the first column of the table array is text and the lookup value is a number. You can see an example of this in the file 04_Text_and_numbers.

1. Highlight the range A3:A16 in the Text Part sheet and then look at the dropdown in the Number section of the Home tab. You can see that it is formatted as Text (see Figure 4-11).

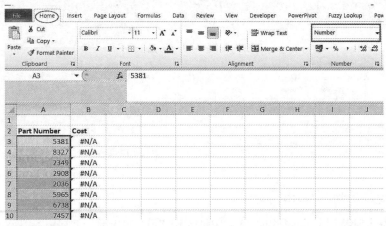

Figure 4-11

2. Highlight the range A3:A16 in the Number Part sheet and then look at the dropdown in the Number section of the Home tab. You can see that it is formatted as Number (see Figure 4-12).

Figure 4-12

3. Look at the Vlookup() function in B3:B16 in the Number Part sheet. You can see that the function has returned #N/A errors, even though the Part Number entries look identical for both the entries in A3:A16 in the Number sheet and A3:A16 in the Text sheet.

4. Correct the #N/A errors by converting Part Number for both sheets to the same data type (e.g., Text or Number).

5. If step 4 doesn't work, in the Text Part sheet, highlight the range A3:A16, click the yellow exclamation point, and choose Convert to Number (see Figure 4-13).

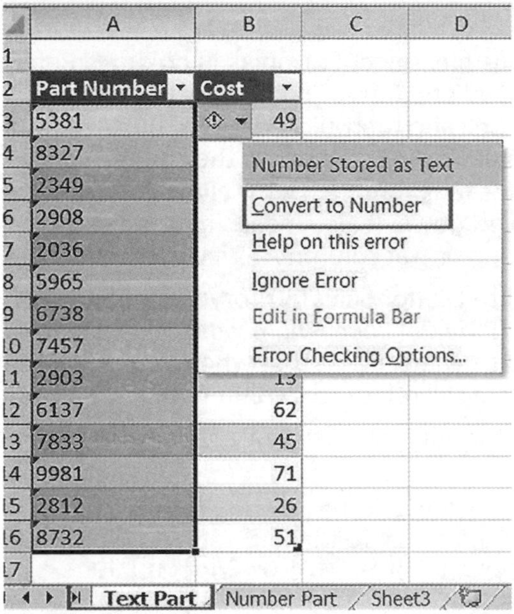

Figure 4-13

Removing Extra Spaces

Excel and all other programs (and computers themselves) see a space as a character, so one thing you might need to check is that you have the same number of spaces in both the lookup value and the matching entry in the first column of a table array.

If you don't have the same number of spaces, you may have to use the Trim() function, which you have already seen in Chapter 2.

Fixing the Lookup Value When You Need to Pull in a Lot of Columns

Just a little while ago, I said that you need to copy in one set of data (i.e., SalesTerritoryRegion). But let's say you have to copy in the data for SalesTerritoryCountry and SalesTerritoryGroup as well. Also assume that you need to work across two files, 04_Sales_territories and 04_Vlookup_functions_files. Of course, you could just enter the function again and again, but there's another way:

1. Make sure the following files are open: 04_Sales_territories and 04_Vlookup_functions files.

2. If you have not done so already, in the 04_Vlookup_functions file, click in B2 and enter your Vlookup() formula to pull in SalesTerritoryRegion.

3. Go to the next heading by clicking in cell C2 and enter a Vlookup() function to pull in SalesTerritoryCountry.

4. In the 04_Vlookup_functions file, select Formulas | Lookup & Reference | VLOOKUP and then, in the Function Arguments dialog, when you have clicked in Lookup_value box and then clicked on A2, press F4 until you get the following configuration: $A2. (This fixes the column so that your Vlookup() will always refer to column A, but it allows the rows to change as the function is copied down. It also means that it is tethered to column A so that it's always looking at column A as it is copied across.)

5. Copy across your Vlookup() to D2 (for SalesTerritoryGroup) and then amend your Vlookup() in D2 so the *Col_index_num* value is 4 instead of 3. It updates to show the correct value. (Note that when you check the function in C2, the *Lookup_value* still references column A.)

6. Repeat step 5 for SalesTerritoryAlternateKey but change the *Col_index_num* value to 5.

> **Note** Of course, another tweak would be to add column numbers above your table array and refer to them in your Vlookup(). You can see an example of this in the file 04_Vlookup_function_column_with_numbers, which references 04_Sales_territories_with_numbers. Note how the column numbers have been entered into B1:E1 in the 04_Sales_territories_with_numbers file. You use these numbers instead of entering them into the *Col_index_num* part of the function. In this case, in the *Col_index_num* part of the Vlookup(), you enter the cell that has the column number (in the Sales territories with numbers file) but configure it (using F4) to show C$1.

> **Survival Tip** If you open 04_Vlookup_function_column_with_numbers without having 04_Sales_territories_with_numbers open, you see REF! instead of the values. The good news is that when you open the file, the correct values appear.

Using Vlookup() to Identify New Entries

One very common scenario is that product lists or nominal ledger codes are added from a previous month. When this happens, you need to identify what new entries you have that you didn't have in the previous month.

1. Ensure that you have these two files open: 04_This_month_file and 04_Last_month_file.

2. In the 04_This_month_file workbook, add the new column heading Last Month in cell E1.

3. In cell E2, enter a Vlookup() that looks up the matching account number against the 04_Last_month_file workbook and returns the matching amount.

4. Click in E2 and select Formulas | Lookup & Reference | VLOOKUP.

5. Click on B2. [@Account] appears in the Lookup_value box in the Function Arguments dialog.

6. Click in the *Table_array* part of the Vlookup() function.

7. Go to the 04_Last_month file and highlight columns A to D. Note that Excel gives you the table reference '04 Last month file. xlsx'!Table1[#All].

8. Enter 4 in the Col_index_num box.

9. Enter FALSE for Range_lookup.

10. Click OK. Because the data is formatted as a table, it copies down automatically to the end of the range (row 642) in the 04_This_month_file.

11. Look at cells E641 and E642, and you see #N/A in both of them, indicating two new entries. The two new account entries in the 04_This_ month file appear as #N/A because while they are account entries in the 04_This_month file, they are not entries in the 04_Last_month file. Because these are brand-new accounts (i.e., they did not exist in previous months), the best solution would be to add an Iferror() function around the Vlookup() that says "no match" or 0. This would make these new entries easier to identify.

> **Note** You can find this completed file in 04_This_month_file_ with_solution. It includes an Iferror() function to return 0 (zero) instead of #N/A.

Determining Whether You Need a Helper Cell and Adding One if You Do

To use a Vlookup() function, you need to have a matching column in both your lookup value and table array. You also need the lookup value to be a unique value.

In the examples in this chapter, you have had SalesTerritoryKey in both files. If you are using something like a barcode, that number will be both on your product and in the file with all the data you want to pull in. But that is not always the case. Let's look at an example.

Say that you want to combine the quantity, price, invoice numbers, and product names for each of these products into one file. In one file, 04_FileA (see Table 4-1), you have the invoice number, product number, and quantity; this is on the sheet called 04_FileA. In the other file, 04_FileB (see Table 4-2), you have invoice number, product number, and product price.

Table 4-1: 04_FileA

Invoice Number	Product Name	Quantity
100	A	5000
100	C	1000
200	A	350

Table 4-2: 04_FileB

Invoice Number	Product Name	Price
100	A	200
100	B	300
200	A	500

What you want to do is link the two files together to get a total. However, neither the invoice number on its own nor the product number on its own is unique, so you can't use a Vlookup() with the data as it is currently presented. So, what can you do?

The solution is to create a "helper cell" that will provide you with a unique identifier. You can create the unique identifier by using concatenation to combine the invoice number and the product name. This will be the field you then use to do the comparison.

You need to ensure that the helper cells are the same in both files and are the same data type (either text or numbers). You also need to make sure the helper cell is the first column in the table array part of the formula.

Follow these steps to create the helper cell:

1. In 04_FileA, click where you want the helper cell to go (to the left of the first column in cell A2) and type =.

2. Click in the first cell that contains text: B2 (i.e., the one that contains 100 in the Invoice Number column). Type &.

3. Click in cell C2 (i.e., the one that contains A in the Product Name column). You now have a formula that looks like this: =B2&C2.

4. Press Enter to copy down this formula (cell A2 should now read 100A) and to cells A3 and A4.

> **Note** It can often be useful to give the helper cell columns the same name in both sheets.

You can see the solution for 04_FileA on the sheet called 04_FileASolution (see Table 4-3). In this case you used a helper cell (in cells E2:E4) to pull in the price from 04_FileB for the entries with the matching helper cell entry (Invoice Number and Product Name combined).

Table 4-3: 04_FileA (04_FileASolution Sheet)

Helper Cell	Invoice Number	Product Name	Quantity	Price
100A	100	A	5000	200
100C	100	C	1000	300
200A	200	A	350	500

Repeat these steps to create a helper cell for 04_FileB. Table 4-4 shows the example in cell A2 of the 04_FileB_solution sheet. You now have a matching column, so you can use Vlookup() on this data. Check the formula in cell E2 of the 04_FileB_solution sheet to see how this Vlookup() works.

Table 4-4: 04_FileB (04_FileB_solution Sheet)

Helper Cell	Invoice Number	Product Name	Price	Quantity
100A	100	A	200	5000
100C	100	C	300	1000
200A	200	A	500	350

Summary

Now you are familiar with the Vlookup() function. You have seen it in operation in three common situations: matching up data in the same worksheet and file, matching up data in the same file but different worksheets, and matching up data in two different files. You have also had a chance to explore and solve some of the most common problems that arise when using this powerful function, including what to do with different data types, how to clean up extra spaces, and how to fix a column so you can more easily copy the function across to other columns. You have also seen working examples of two common real-life situations: Pulling in matching data from a previous month and using a helper cell.

Chapter 5 Creating Pivot Tables

By now you have collected, massaged, and manipulated your data until it is in pivot-friendly format: Your data is all together, it's accurate, it's normalized, and you have made a table of it. I hope you had a little lie-down before starting this chapter because it's time for pivot tables.

If you need to summarise data or do comparisons—perhaps across months or years—you need to get familiar with pivot tables. Essentially, a pivot table summarizes a list so that you can, for example, get totals by month, by region. You can add these totals, average them, get the max, and get the min if you want to. You can view the numbers as percentages of the grand total. And you can get all these results and more in minutes.

I do believe that most questions in Excel can be answered with a pivot table, which is Excel's primary analysis tool. Or, as a class participant once said to me, "The world of work runs on two things: pivot tables and PowerPoint." And now Power Pivot, which is covered in Chapter 7, "Beyond the Pivot Table: Power Pivot," is starting to gallop up from behind.

This chapter shows you all the basics of using pivot tables to look at data from different angles. You've already done a lot of work prepping your data, but you need to look at it one more time, to make sure it's really ready for a pivot table that will turn it into the information you're looking for.

If you are using Excel 2010 or earlier, all the data you need for a pivot table has to be on one sheet. It's probably a good idea also to filter out any data you don't require. (You've seen filtering already in Chapter 1, "Back to Basics: What Do You Know Already?")

Assembling Data for a Pivot Table

You know how chefs always talk about the importance of fresh, high-quality ingredients? Well, pivot tables also work best with fresh, high-quality ingredients: You need to give pivot tables good, clean data, or you will have a lot of problems on your hands. Before you start messing around with a pivot table, make sure your data meets all the following criteria:

- Normalized so that every transaction has its own row.
- No blank rows or columns.
- Entries in all date columns (If you have a blank cell in your dates and you attempt to group dates together—into months or quarters or years—you will have problems.)

- One heading per cell.
- Consistent data (By *consistent* I mean that all repeating entries should be entered exactly the same way. For example, in Ireland we have a county called Mayo. You as a human know that County Mayo, Co. Mayo, and Mayo are all the same place. Excel doesn't. It thinks they are three different places and will show them as such.)
- No subtotal cells.
- All in one place (You may need to use Vlookup() to make this happen.)
- Converted to a table.

When you're sure your data meets these criteria, you're ready for the fun part. Welcome to pivot tables.

Creating Your First Pivot Table

1. Open the file 05_Pivot_transactions.

2. In the Transactions sheet, click in the table and select Design | Summarize with PivotTable (see Figure 5-1). (Note that if you click outside the table, the Design tab disappears.)

Figure 5-1

3. In the Create PivotTable dialog that appears, accept the default settings (which automatically select the table and assume that you want to put your pivot table on a new worksheet) and click OK.

You now see the PivotTable Field List (see Figure 5-2). The top half of it shows the headings from your data source on the Transactions sheet: Date, Payee, Account, Category, Amount, and Quarter.

> **Note** The headings in this list vary depending on the headings in the data.

At the bottom of the PivotTable Field List you see four areas: Report Filter, Column Labels, Row Labels, and Values. Generally speaking, you put your number field in the Values area (by simply dragging it down from the list of headings), and you need at least one other field to be entered.

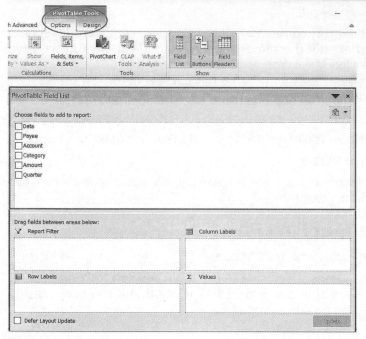

Figure 5-2

> **Survival Tip** People often get hung up on what goes in each of the four areas (i.e., Report Filter, Column Labels, Row Labels, and Values) for a pivot table. In general, you should put dates in the Row Labels area and put whatever it is you want to add/count in the Values area. Don't be afraid to move your fields around. You can have more than one heading in each of the four areas (e.g., you can have the headings Date and Quarter in the Row Labels area).

4. To get a summary by month and category of the amounts, with an option to view by payee, set up a pivot table as follows:

- Drag the Amount heading into the Values area.

- Drag the Payee heading into the Report Filter area.

- Drag the Date heading into the Row Labels area.

- Drag the Category heading into the Column Labels area.

Figure 5-3 shows the pivot table that results from making these changes in the PivotTable Field List. (You can also see and play with this in the Pivot 1 sheet of the 05_Pivot_transactions_with_solutions file.) You now have a list of individual days on the left, with the category headings going across the top and lots of numbers scattered across.

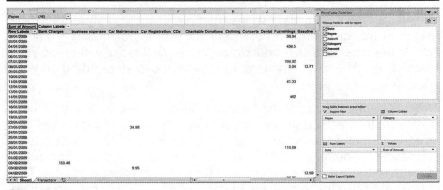

Figure 5-3

5. Grouping by months would help the data in this pivot table make more sense, so right-click in the dates and select Group. Then, in the Grouping dialog that appears, select Months. If you need to include Years in your grouping, you can do so now by clicking on Years. Both appear selected (see Figure 5-4). The data starts to look better right away.

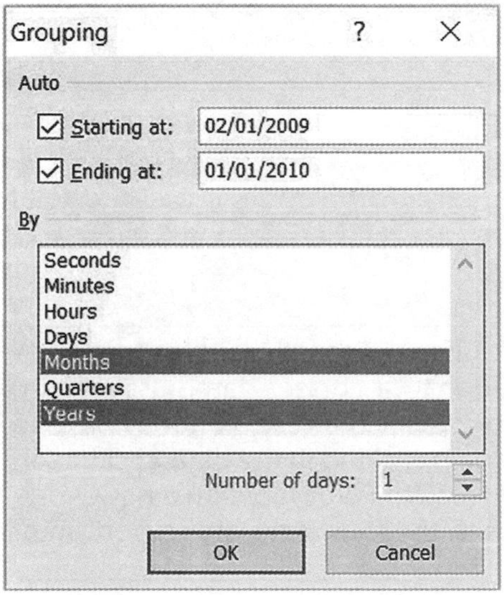

Figure 5-4

Survival Tips If your data spans multiple years, you should include Years in this grouping. Otherwise, your months or quarters will include the data from all months/quarters, regardless of years—so your results could be very very good or very very bad, depending on your data set.

Also, sometimes you get the message Cannot group by that selection. This usually means that one of your dates is blank or incorrectly formatted. Amend the incorrect date. If there is no date specified for a transaction, you may need to enter a dummy date (e.g., the first of the month or the last of the month) and then refresh your pivot table. This error could also mean that you have highlighted the entire worksheet instead of just the table for your pivot table preparation. In that case, simply select only the table and create the pivot table again.

6. To ensure that your pivot table reflects the most up-to-date version of the data, refresh the data by right-clicking in the Values section (the data part of the pivot table) and choosing Refresh (see Figure 5-5).

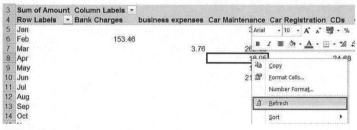

Figure 5-5

Survival Tip Note that sometimes if you have a blank or incorrectly formatted date and you amend it to a correct date, just refreshing does not correct the pivot table. In such a case, you may have to re-create the pivot table by once again clicking in the data, clicking on the Design tab, choosing Summarize with Pivot Table on a new worksheet, and dragging the headings to the four areas at the bottom of the PivotTable Field List.

Understanding Summarize Values By

You might have noticed above that when you dragged the Amount heading down to the Values area, Excel automatically changed Amount to Sum of Amount. That's because Excel assumes that what you usually want to do with your values is to add them up. Usually the Values area setting you need is in "Sum of" format (i.e., adding). However, you may want to do other summaries of your values, such as show the highest

(Max), the lowest (Min), the average (Average), or the quantity (Count). You have nearly a dozen options here, and in this section you'll see how to change the main ones.

Let's say you currently have a sum of sales, but you want to get the average of sales. It's easy to change your pivot table so it shows an average instead of a sum: Click somewhere in Values part of the pivot table, right-click, and select Summarize Values By | Average (see Figure 5-6).

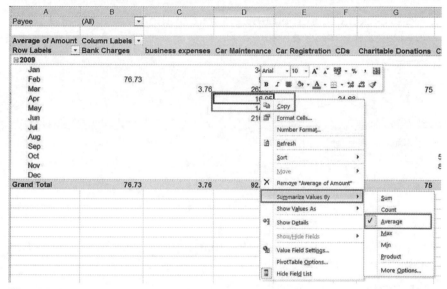

Figure 5-6

Survival Tip Sometimes when you add to the Values area columns that contain numbers, Excel gives you Count instead of Sum. This is usually because Excel doesn't recognise some of the numbers in the column as numbers. Excel is trying to be helpful in assuming that you want to use Count rather than Sum because it sees the values as text rather than as numbers. In this case, you may need to reformat the entire column in the original table as numbers. However, a technique I have found that often seems to prevent this problem is to add a column to the Values area first before adding column headings to the other areas of the PivotTable Field List.

Note If you check out the Pivot 2 worksheet in the file 05_Pivot_transactions_with_solutions, you can see these five options for Summarize Values By: Sum, Count, Average, Max, and Min.

Tidying Up the Numbers in a Pivot Table

You might have already noticed that the numbers in the Pivot 1 pivot table you've just created are not formatted as currency. You might be tempted to change this by using the Format Cells option on the Home tab. Don't do that, though, or you'll make a lot of extra work for yourself. Instead, you use the number formatting options that come with pivot tables, as described here:

1. Right-click a cell in the numbers part of the pivot table and select Value Field Settings (see Figure 5-7).

Figure 5-7

2. In the Value Field Settings dialog that appears, click the Number Format button (see Figure 5-8).

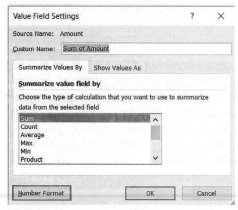

Figure 5-8

3. In the Format Cells dialog that appears, choose the appropriate number format—in this case, Currency—and click OK and then click OK again. Excel uses the currency format for all the numbers in the pivot table related to that particular heading in the Values area.

> **Survival Tip** When you update the number format, the change affects just the numbers from the same column. If you have multiple column headings in the Values area of the PivotTable Field List and want to update the number formats for other columns, you need to do so separately for each one.

Refreshing Data in a Pivot Table

When you make changes to the data in a pivot table, either by changing existing entries or adding new rows or columns, these changes are not automatically reflected in the pivot table. If you have converted a data source to a table, all you have to do is click in the pivot table and select Options | Refresh to bring in the most up-to-date data. If you can't see the Options tab, make sure you have clicked in the pivot table and look all the way down on the right side of the ribbon.

> **Note** Under Options | Refresh, you can select Refresh All if you want to update multiple pivot tables at once.

Although it is recommended that you convert a list to a table before making it into a pivot table, you don't actually have to do so. If a pivot table is not based on a table and the data now has added new columns or rows, you update it by selecting Options | Change Data Source (see Figure 5-9) and then highlight the new data.

Figure 5-9

Refreshing the data in a pivot table that's not based on a table isn't too problematic if you only have a small data source, but it's very tedious with the large data sets that are becoming increasingly common. So do yourself a favour and turn your data into a table before converting it to a pivot table.

Grouping by Dates

One of the "oooh!" moments for a lot of people in my Excel classes is when I show them how to group by dates. (A student once pronounced it "groping by dates," but I explained that that's a *whole* different class.)

Excel lets you easily group by quarters, which it defines as the standard quarters (January–March, Quarter 1; April–June, Quarter 2; July–September, Quarter 3; and October–December, Quarter 4).

Of course, Excel understands that your fiscal year might run a bit differently than the traditional one, and it allows you to redefine the quarters. One way to do this is to add an extra column to your table called Quarter and reference a sheet that shows the months allocated to your fiscal year. In the following steps, assume that the first month of the fiscal year is April (month 4):

1. Open the file called 05_Pivot_transactions_with_solutions.

2. Navigate to the worksheet Transactions Without Quarters. Also in this work (05_Pivot_transactions_with_solutions), find the sheet called Months that already has the Quarters table created in it (see Table 5-1).

Table 5-1: Quarters Table in the Months Sheet

Month	Quarter
1	4
2	4
3	4
4	1
5	1
6	1
7	2
8	2
9	2
10	3
11	3

3. In the worksheet Transactions Without Quarters, add the heading Quarters in cell F1.

4. In the new Quarters column, type the following formula:

```
=Vlookup(Month([@Date]),quarters,2,FALSE)
```

Excel puts in the quarter number for you. The formula automatically copies down because this data has been set up as a table.

Grouping by Amounts

Another cool feature that helps with data analysis is grouping by quantities. For example, if you want to see the total value of sales where the total invoice amount is in a certain range, you can group your sales quantities into bands (e.g., 0–5000, 5001–10000, 10001–15000). The following example assumes that you want to group the Amount field into increments of 10, starting at 0 and ending at 1000:

1. Open the file called 05_Pivot_transactions_with_solutions

2. Follow the same steps as earlier to create a pivot table.

3. Add the Amount heading to the Values area of the PivotTable Field List.

4. Add the Amount heading to the Row Labels area. Excel creates a pivot table for you.

5. Right-click in the Row Labels area data in the pivot table and select Group.

6. In the Grouping dialog that appears, set Starting At to 0, set Ending At to 1000, and set By to 10 (see Figure 5-10).

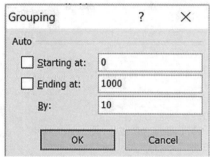

Figure 5-10

The Grouping worksheet in the 05_Pivot_transactions_with_solutions file shows an example of the pivot table that results from these changes.

> **Note** You can also sort Sum of Amount in ascending order by right-clicking in the field and selecting Sort | Largest to Smallest.

Showing Values As

Quite often you need to show the numbers you already have in a pivot table in a different way. And quite often Excel provides just the setting you need in the pivot table. You can either apply the setting you want to the numbers you have added to the Values area of the PivotTable Field

List or you can add a field to Values again and then apply the settings you need to the second iteration.

To see the available options, right-click the numbers field in your pivot table that you want to change and select Show Values As. As shown in Figure 5-11, you get 15 options in this list (gulp). The following sections focus on the ones that are used most often.

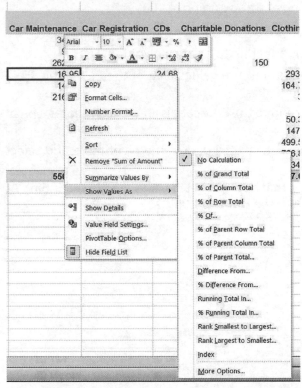

Figure 5-11

Note It can be a very useful exercise to just add the same field again to the Values area of the PivotTable Field List and experiment with the various options there just to get a feel for the answers the various options give you.

The Pivot 3 sheet in the file 05_Pivot_transactions_with_solutions shows the following four options:

Note You can get these results by right-clicking Amount in the PivotTable Field List, selecting Value Field Settings, and then changing the Custom Name setting at the top of the Value Field Settings dialog (see Figure 5-12).

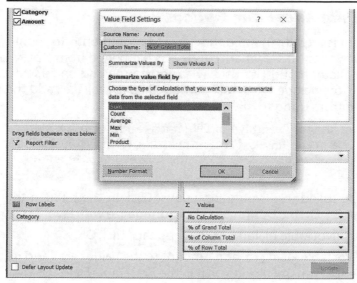

Figure 5-12

- **No Calculation:** This option is the default and shows you the numbers in the Sum/Average/Count format you have already specified under Summarize Values By. If you open the Pivot 3 sheet in the 05_Pivot_transactions_with_solutions file and look at cell B4, you can see that the total for Bank Charges was 153.46.

- **% of Grand Total:** This option shows what percentage each figure is of the total. This is useful if you want to get a global look at your data. The grand total number at the end adds up all the other figures to 100%. The number that is 153.46 with No Calculation selected is now 0.27%, which is the percentage of the total (bank charges are 153.40 divided by the total 57170, which you can see in cell B33 in the Pivot 3 sheet in the 05_Pivot_transactions_with_solutions file).

- **% of Column Total:** This option allows you to show the percentage breakdown headings for the columns. Each *column* adds up to 100%. Therefore, 153.46 divided by the total of this column (still 57170) is also 0.27%.

- **% of Row Total:** This option allows you to show the percentage breakdown headings for the rows. Each *row* adds up to 100%. In the example shown in the Pivot 3 sheet in the file 05_Pivot_transactions_with_solutions, because nothing is added to the Row Labels area of the PivotTable Field List, % of Row Total shows up as 100%. If you add Payee to the Row Labels area, these results change (although you have to scroll right across the screen to see them).

Using the Difference From Option

Difference From is a really useful option for showing month-to-month changes. It allows you to see what change has happened from a previous month or a later month. It's usually easiest to see and understand the changes if you include the actual number field as well (i.e., add the number field you are using to the Values area again).

> **Note** I have shown examples of Difference From in the sheet called Pivot 4 in the file 05_Pivot_transactions_with_solutions because it's easier to follow when it's shown on a separate sheet.

1. Open the file called 05_Pivot_transactions. Click in the table in the Transactions sheet. On the Design tab, click Summarize with Pivot Table.

2. In the Create PivotTable dialog box that appears, click OK.

3. Using the PivotTable Field List, add Amount to the Values area and rename it Difference From by clicking on it in the PivotTable Field List area, navigating to Value Field Settings, and changing the Custom Name setting to Difference From (see Figure 5-13). Also make sure it is using Sum rather than Count.

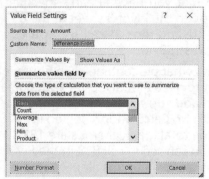

Figure 5-13

> **Note** If you see that Excel is using Count rather than Sum for summarizing the data, change it in the Value Field Settings dialog, as shown in Figure 5-14.

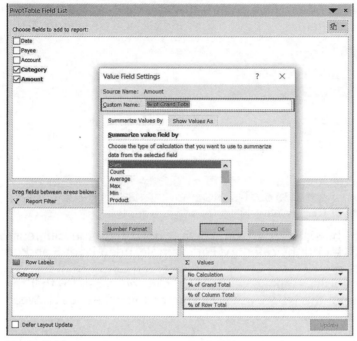

Figure 5-14

4. Add Amount to the Values area of the PivotTable Field List again.

5. Add Quarter to the Column Labels area.

6. Add Category to the Row Labels area.

7. Right-click the Difference From field in the pivot table and choose Show Values As | Difference From (see Figure 5-15).

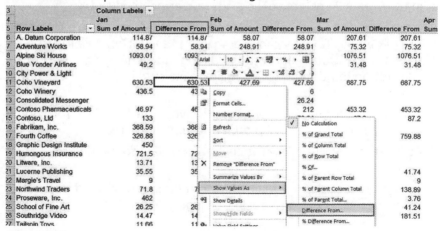

Figure 5-15

8. In the Show Values As dialog, change the Base Field setting to `Quarter`, change Base Item to `(previous)`, and click OK (see Figure 5-16).

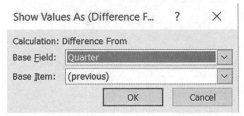

Figure 5-16

> **Note** In order to get the fields to sit side by side in the pivot table, you may need to put Quarter above Values in the Column Labels area of the PivotTable Field List.

The figures in the Difference From column now show the difference from month to month by category. For example, open Pivot 5 and go to cell A8 where you will see Car Maintenance. You can see that the January value for this is 34.98 (in cell B8). You can see in cell D8 that the February value for this is 9.95. In cell E8 you see the difference between these two values, which is −25.03.

Using the Running Totals Option

Running Totals is an option that accountants love. It shows cumulative balances. You can see an example of this option in the Pivot 5 sheet in the file 05_Pivot_transactions_with_solutions.

1. Click in the table in the Transactions sheet and select Design | Summarize with Pivot Table.

2. In the Create PivotTable dialog box that appears, click OK.

3. Add Amount to the Values area of the PivotTable Field List and rename it Running Total by clicking on it in the PivotTable Field List area, navigating to Value Field Settings dialog, and changing the Custom Name setting to Running Total. Again, make sure it is using Sum rather than Count.

4. Add Amount to the Values area of the PivotTable Field List. You should now have two instances of Amount in your Values area.

5. Add Category to the Row Labels area and Date to the Column Labels area.

6. In the pivot table, right-click in the Running Total field and select Show Values As | Running Total In (see Figure 5-17).

Figure 5-17

7. In the Show Values As (Running Total) dialog, set Base Field to `Date` (see Figure 5-18).

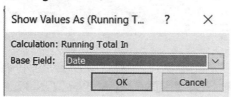

Figure 5-18

Now when you view the data (in the worksheet Pivot 5) you see that the numbers have been added up month on month. For example, for Car Maintenance, check the running total for February (44.93 in cell E8) and notice that it is made up of the January (34.98 in cell B8) and February (9.95 in cell D8) numbers.

> **Survival Tip** Notice that if you highlight the numbers you want to add together and view the status bar in the bottom-left corner, you can ensure that the numbers add up. For example, if you highlight cell C8 (34.98) and cell D8 (9.95) and check the status bar, you see 44.93, which is the running total given in cell E8 for Car Maintenance.

Using Report Filters

So far in this chapter, you have formatted numbers to currency and grouped dates. You have also seen a number of different ways to present values. This section looks at report filters, which allow you to filter pivot tables based on specific headings (e.g., Payee, Category).

In the Pivot 6 sheet in the file 05_Pivot_transactions_with_solutions, you can see that Payees has been added to the Report Filters area of the PivotTable Field List. If you click on the Payees heading, you get a dropdown list of the payees. If you click one of the payees, you see the pivot table data change to reflect just that payee. If you want to see two or more payees together, select the Select Multiple Items check box (see Figure 5-19). You can then select the payees whose data you want to see reflected in the pivot table.

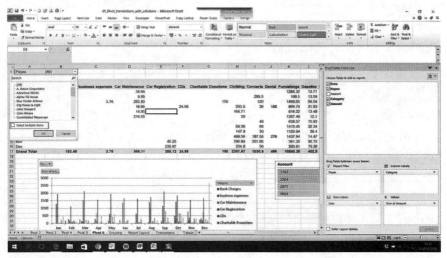

Figure 5-19

There is another useful thing you can do with the Report Filters option. I discovered this feature on one of Mike Alexander's videos (see www.datapigtechnologies.com), and it's really helpful. Let's say you have to generate a pivot table for every payee. Now that's not too bad if you have only 1 or 2 payees, but let's say you have 20 or 30 payees. You'd be facing a lot of work. But there is a way around that work:

1. Click in your pivot table and select Options | Options.

2. In the Options dialog that appears, select Report Filter Pages, select Payee, and click OK.

Presto! You have just created an instant pivot table for each payee. You still have the original, too, so you've lost nothing.

> **Note** The one drawback with this method is that if you have created charts with the first pivot table, Excel doesn't propagate the charts to the other payees. So if you have used charts, unfortunately, you will have to re-create them.

Setting Up Slicers (but Only if You Have Excel 2010 or Later)

When I show how to set up slicers in class, users love it. Slicers are—dare I say it—one of the best things since sliced bread. This feature, which debuted in Excel 2010, allows you to slice and dice your data in real time—and if you have a chart, a slicer works there, too.

1. Open the Pivot 6 sheet in the file 05_Pivot_transactions_with_solutions.

2. Click on the pivot table and select PivotTable Tools Options | Insert Slicer | Insert Slicer (see Figure 5-20).

Figure 5-20

3. In the slicer, choose what you want the headings in the pivot table to link it to. For example, you could click on Account for the slicer. Or try choosing multiple headings by holding down Ctrl as you click the headings you want. Watch how the pivot table data changes to reflect your choices.

4. To clear all the filters, click the Clear Filter icon on the top-right side of the filter (see Figure 5-21).

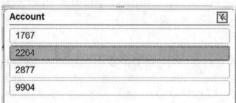

Figure 5-21

5. If you want to add another slicer, simply repeat step 2 and choose a different heading to slice your data by.

6. To use one slicer for multiple pivot tables, click on one of the pivot tables and select Slicer Tools Options | PivotTable Connections. Then, in the PivotTable Connections dialog, select the box for the pivot table you want to connect the slicer to (see Figure 5-22).

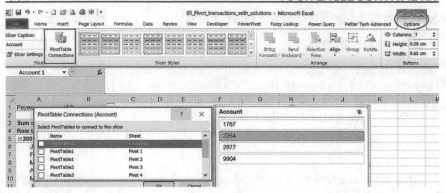

Figure 5-22

7. To change the look of your slicers, choose from the Slicer Styles portion of the Slicer Tools Options tab (see Figure 5-23). (Note that this tab becomes visible only when you click on a slicer.)

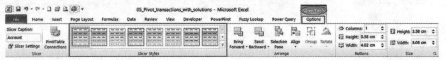

Figure 5-23

8. Slicers don't tend to autofit, so to adjust, use the Height option on the Slicer Tools Options tab (see Figure 5-24) to resize a slicer to the desired height.

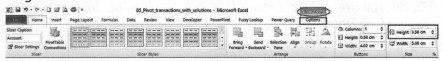

Figure 5-24

9. To get the headings to go across the slicer, use the Buttons area of the Slicer Tools Options tab (see Figure 5-25). For example, if you choose 3 for Columns, you get three headings laid horizontally across your slicer, whereas if you choose 1, you see just one heading at a time.

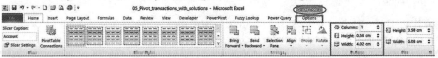

Figure 5-25

If you have a chart, the slicer settings also apply to the chart, and you can see your data and chart change dynamically depending on what options you select in the slicer. You can also use the slicer settings to remove the headings and borders to give yourself more space. This is particularly handy if you are using a slicer for something like a dashboard.

Changing Pivot Table Layout

Excel offers a variety of layouts for pivot tables. To experiment with the different layouts available, select the Design tab and try out the options on the left side.

Removing/Adding Subtotals

Say that you don't want to see subtotals in your pivot table. Often subtotals are meaningless because they're based on columns in the Values area that just don't lend themselves to subtotalling. Excel offers a few options for subtotals.

1. Open the Report Layout sheet of the 05_Pivot_transactions_with_ solutions file, which has a pivot table already set up for you to experiment on.

2. To remove the subtotals from this pivot table, click in the pivot table and select PivotTable Tools Design | Subtotals | Do Not Show Subtotals (see Figure 5-26).

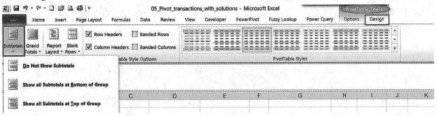

Figure 5-26

3. To have subtotals show at the top, click in the pivot table and select PivotTable Tools Design | Subtotals | Show All Subtotals at Top of Group.

4. To have subtotals show at the bottom, click in the pivot table and select PivotTable Tools Design | Subtotals | Show All Subtotals at Bottom of Group.

Experiment with the various options to see what effects they have.

Removing/Adding Grand Totals

Like subtotals, grand totals are sometimes essential for the data you want to convey. Other times, they are not. Excel gives you several options for dealing with them.

1. Open the Report Layout sheet of the 05_Pivot_transactions_with_ solutions file, which has a pivot table already set up for you to experiment on.

2. Click in the pivot table and select PivotTable Tools Design | Grand Totals (see Figure 5-27).

3. Experiment with the four options in the Grand Totals menu to see what the pivot table looks like with the grand totals on and off for rows and totals.

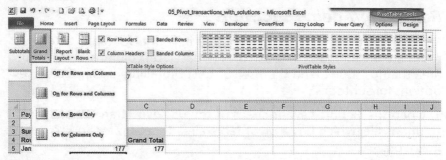

Figure 5-27

Changing the Report Layout

If you select PivotTable Tools Design | Report Layout, you see the following options (see Figure 5-28):

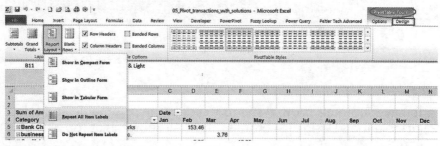

Figure 5-28

- **Show in Compact Form:** This option is the default.

- **Show in Outline Form:** This option tends to create more columns for your data.

- **Show in Tabular Form:** This option yields the layout form much beloved by experienced Excel users. It lays out the data in a horizontal form rather than the more stepped format of Compact form and Outline form.

Note that if you use Tabular form and want to see your headings repeated, you need to select the Repeat All Items Labels option. Figure 5-29 shows what this looks like, and you can check out the Tabular Layout Repeating Items sheet in the 05_Pivot_transactions_with_solutions file to get a closer look.

3	Sum of Amount	
4	Category ▼	Payee ▼
5	⊟Bank Charges	Adventure Works
6	⊟business expenses	Proseware, Inc.
7	⊟Car Maintenance	Alpine Ski House
8	Car Maintenance	Litware, Inc.
9	Car Maintenance	Trey Research
10	⊟Car Registration	The Phone Company
11	⊟CDs	City Power & Light
12	⊟Charitable Donations	A. Datum Corporation
13	Charitable Donations	Adventure Works
14	⊟Clothing	A. Datum Corporation
15	Clothing	Alpine Ski House
16	Clothing	Coho Vineyard
17	Clothing	Consolidated Messenger
18	Clothing	Contoso, Ltd
19	Clothing	Fabrikam, Inc.
20	Clothing	Fourth Coffee
21	Clothing	Humongous Insurance
22	Clothing	Lucerne Publishing
23	Clothing	Proseware, Inc.
24	Clothing	School of Fine Art
25	Clothing	Tailspin Toys
26	Clothing	Trey Research
27	Clothing	Woodgrove Bank

Figure 5-29

Seeing What's Behind the Numbers

In my experience, most accountants love matching balances. I've also noticed that they love being able to see what makes up the numbers. Excel accommodates accountants—and the rest of us—by making it easy to find out what's behind the numbers: Just double-click a number in a pivot table, and Excel shows you the full list of transactions that make up that number.

Sometimes, though, you try this, and Excel holds on to the secret. If that happens to you, follow these steps:

1. Select PivotTable Tools Options | Options.

2. In the PivotTable Options dialog that appears, select the Data tab.

3. Make sure the Enable Show Details check box is ticked (see Figure 5-30).

Figure 5-30

Putting Zeros in Blank Cells

Scientists have pointed out to me that a blank is not the same as a zero. But sometimes you want zeros to appear in a worksheet instead of blanks if only to show that you know zero happened. Follow these steps to put zeros in blank cells:

1. Click in a pivot table. You could use the pivot table in the Report Layout sheet of the 05_Pivot_transactions_with_solutions file.

2. Choose PivotTable Tools Options | Options.

3. In the PivotTable Options dialog that appears, select the Layout & Format tab (see Figure 5-31).

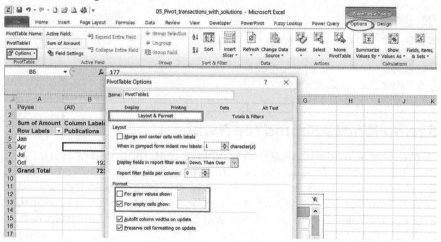

Figure 5-31

4. Choose the For Empty Cells Show check box and then enter 0 (or whatever else you want to appear instead of empty cells).

> **Note** In the Layout & Format tab you can also choose what you want to appear instead of the default error values. For example, you might want to enter something like No Value.

Adding a Chart

Pivot tables are so incredibly useful. It's now time to talk about their charting features—especially the filtering options, which allow you to filter in situ as you add and remove filters.

1. Click in a pivot table (such as any of the pre-created pivot tables in the 05_Pivot_transactions_with_solutions file) and select PivotTable Tools Options | Pivot Chart. The Insert Chart dialog appears (see Figure 5-32),

and you can see that it looks very similar to the dialog you use for creating an ordinary chart (as discussed in Chapter 1).

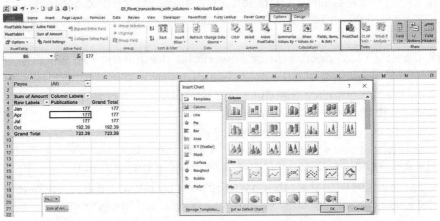

Figure 5-32

2. In the Insert Chart dialog, choose the Column tab and then select the first option under Column: Clustered Column. Excel creates a clustered column chart for you, based on your data.

> **Note** The Pivot 1 sheet in the file 05_Pivot_transactions_with_ solutions shows an example of a clustered column chart based on a pivot table.

The main difference between Excel's usual charts and pivot charts is that pivot charts include filtering options. So, for example, if you click the Category button on a chart, you can filter the chart. When you do that, you also filter the contents of the pivot table.

> **Note** You can remove the filter icons from a chart by clicking in the chart and selecting PivotChart Tools Analyze | Field Buttons and then selecting one of the four options shown in Figure 5-33, depending on what you want to hide or show. If you hide them all by clicking Hide All and want to restore them, click in the chart, select PivotChart Tools Analyze | Field Buttons, and then deselect the Hide All option at the bottom.

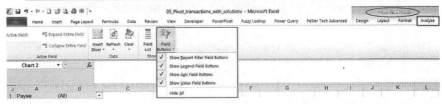

Figure 5-33

Adding a Chart to Word or PowerPoint

Once you have created a data set, often the next step is to get that data into a Word document or a PowerPoint presentation. Follow these steps to try it yourself:

1. Open a Word document or PowerPoint presentation to which you want to add a chart.

2. In Excel, right-click the chart you want to add to the document or presentation and select Copy.

3. Navigate to the point in the Word document or PowerPoint presentation where you want to paste the chart, right-click, and choose Paste. The Excel chart is pasted into the document or presentation.

4. Experiment with the other paste options by clicking the arrow below the Paste icon and resting your mouse on each of the options:

- Keep Source Formatting
- Use Destination Styles
- Link and Keep Source Formatting
- Link and Use Destination Styles
- Picture
- Keep Text Only

As you hover over each option, Word/PowerPoint gives you a preview of what that choice would look like with your chart to help you decide what best suits your requirements.

> **Survival Tip** Two of these options—Link and Keep Source Formatting and Link and Use Destination Styles—retain a link to the original data, so if any changes are made, those changes are reflected in the chart in your Word document or PowerPoint presentation.

Adding Animation to a Chart in PowerPoint

If you add an Excel chart to PowerPoint, you can add animation to it as described here.

1. In PowerPoint, click on the chart and select Animations | Fly In (see Figure 5-34).

Figure 5-34

2. Click Animations | Animation Pane. The Animation Pane window now appears on the right (see Figure 5-35).

Figure 5-35

3. In the Animation Pane window, make sure your chart is selected and then choose Effect Options from the dropdown (see Figure 5-36).

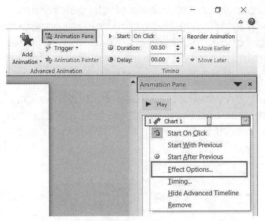

Figure 5-36

4. In the Fly In dialog that appears, select the Chart Animation tab and from the dropdown, choose how you want the data to appear on the chart (see Figure 5-37).

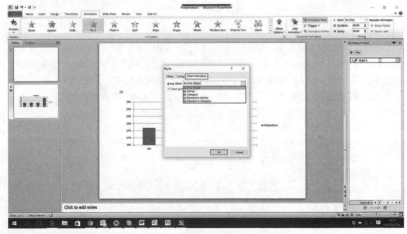

Figure 5-37

The level of detail you get depends on the type of chart chosen. You can also select (or deselect) the box Start Animation by Drawing the Chart Background.

Note You can also construct a chart from scratch within PowerPoint, but this book assumes that your starting point is Excel.

Adding Conditional Formatting

Conditional formatting can be a really powerful final touch for a pivot table. It quickly generates the visual images so beloved by many managers. Conditional formatting allows you to use colour to quickly identify numbers that are at the higher or lower end of the Values spectrum. For example, you can set up conditional formatting to show higher numbers in red and lower numbers in green. The intensity of the colour indicates how close to either end of the Values spectrum a number is.

1. To assign a colour depending on whether a value is high or low, click on one of the values in a pivot table and then select Home | Conditional Formatting | Color Scales (see Figure 5-38). A grey icon appears beside the value.

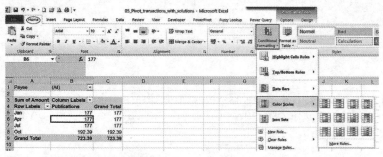

Figure 5-38

2. Click the grey icon that appears beside the value and choose the third value down, which should be something like All Cells Showing *Quantity* for *Whatever Is in Row Labels* and *Whatever Is in Column Labels* (see Figure 5-39). Excel decides what colours to assign to what values.

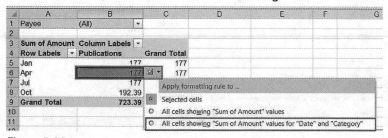

Figure 5-39

3. To see what Excel's underlying assumptions are, choose Home | Conditional Formatting| Manage Rules and look at the rules Excel has applied.

4. Remove the conditional formatting by clicking in the pivot table and choosing Home | Conditional Formatting| Clear Rules | Clear Rules from This PivotTable.

Troubleshooting Pivot Tables

Certain things make your life easier with pivot tables. First of all, you need clean data: no blank rows, no blank columns, one heading per cell. (Have I mentioned this?) Also, you need to have all your pivot data in one place—that is, on one worksheet unless you are using Excel 2013 or later. However, in order to assemble all the required data in one place, you may need to pull in data from other sources by using your (by now beloved) Vlookup().

> **Note** If you open the file 05_Pivot_data_with_vlookups, you can see an example of a data source that has pulled in data from other sources via Vlookup()s.

In addition, if all your data is in a table, all you have to do is click Refresh on your pivot table to update it when the underlying data changes.

> **Note** In Excel 2013 you can pull in data from multiple tables, but in Excel 2010, you can have only one data source.

Alas, the path of pivot tables (like love) doesn't always run smoothly. This section talks about some areas to check if you find that a pivot table isn't working as expected:

- Watch your formatting, especially with dates. Usually if you have problems with your dates—such as getting the dreaded Cannot group by that selection error message—it's because of the formatting. Make sure you have an entry for every cell in your date column and that you don't have impossible dates, such as 30 February or 31 June.

- Watch for dates entered as text instead of as dates. (Check your lists for the green triangles.)

- Ensure that there are no extra spaces in entries for rows and columns. Use validation lists to ensure clean data entry and use the Trim() function to clean up extra spaces.

- Make sure to have your formatting done, complete with formulas, before you construct pivot tables. If you add columns after you have created a pivot table, the pivot table feature will not always pick up the new columns.

- Have you tried turning it off and on again? If a pivot table doesn't work, surprisingly frequently, just re-creating the pivot table works.

- Use tables to avoid having to faff around making sure you have the correct data selected. Once you add new data to a table, usually all you have to do is refresh the pivot table to get the new results.

- When creating a pivot table, remember to add a field to the Values area of the PivotTable Field List first. This really seems to reduce the incidence of problems related to values coming in as Count instead of Sum. (Strange, I know.)

- Have all your data on one sheet. The temptation is often to separate it out by month, but when your boss asks you for the annual figures (and he or she will), it will be much easier to produce that answer from a pivot table that has *all* your data in it.

Summary

If you want to survive and thrive in an Excel world, you need to be familiar with pivot tables. In fact, I am going to go out on a limb and say that you should consider falling in love with pivot tables because they are going to save you massive amounts of time, and after a while, you will find yourself enjoying the exciting things they allow you to do with your data.

Chapter 6 Using Power Query to Quickly Clean Up Data

Power Query is a new add-in for Excel 2010 (and later) that is, quite simply, going to revolutionise your data clean-up tasks. There's not room in this book to cover Power Query in great depth, but this chapter describes how to use it for three frequent data clean-up tasks.

> **Note** A lot of the inspiration I got for this chapter came from attending Ken Puls's talk at the Excel MVP conference in Amsterdam in April 2015.

As you've heard throughout this book, if you want to do any sort of data analysis, your data needs to be clean. That is, it can have no blank rows and no blank columns, and it needs to be organised in a table. As you've heard so many times in this book, the data needs to be normalized, with one row per transaction and all details completed. This is the Holy Grail state for data.

However, most data downloads (particularly from accounting packages) are not organised like this. They usually have subtotals, extra columns, extra rows, and the double underlines that accountants use to say "THIS is the total." When you get such a download, you may need to spend many hours deleting columns, removing totals, and removing rows—and then you may need to repeat that experience every month (usually at month end, when you're sure to have loads and loads of time).

You've learned a bunch of techniques for getting to the Holy Grail state with your data. Alas, it usually takes a lot of work. But learning to use Power Query can help you eliminate most of that work. Power Query lets you do that work just once, save the recipe for your secret sauce, and then call up the recipe again the following month or week and throw in the appropriate data. Power Query does the work for you, getting the data at least most of the way to the Holy Grail state.

> **Note** You do not, by default, have Power Query installed. This chapter does not cover how to install Power Query, but you can easily find Power Query and instructions for installing it at the Microsoft site—or you can ask your IT people to install it for you. Don't forget to emphasise that it is free; the IT department generally likes free. The version you use depends on your machine and your version of Office.

Power Query allows you to pull in data from numerous data sources, including Facebook. It also allows you to easily import text/CSV data from a folder—yes, a *folder*!

This chapter focuses on three data clean-up tasks that people often need help with:

- Cleaning up an accounting data dump
- Converting "unpivoted" data to a pivoted format
- Merging data sets

Cleaning Up an Accounting Data Dump

In this section you are going to learn how to clean up a typical accounting file data dump. I have taken a data dump from a QuickBooks sample company file. This dump is very typical of what an accounting package produces when you click the ever-present Send to Excel button.

If you open the file 06_Accounts_data_dump_01, you'll notice straight away that it has a lot of extra blank rows and columns, and you'll see that totals appear here and there. It's definitely *not* pivot table ready. But it is a very typical accounting file that gives a list of sales of products. Unlike the typical accounting files you'll see, though, this list has already been converted to a table.

> **Note** If you plan to use the Power Query work you do here as the basis for future clean-ups, it's important that you convert the entire list you're cleaning up to a table to ensure that Power Query will pick up all the data, even if the new data has more rows than previous months.

Of course, one of the things you want to check is that the data is still the same when you are finished with your clean-up. So you need to take a look at the total before you begin and again at the end. With this example, before you begin the clean-up process, the total amount is 65,010.65 (cell U130) and the total quantity is 128 (cell Q130).

> **Survival Tip** You can quickly navigate to a cell by pressing F5 and typing the cell number in the Reference box. For example, you can press F5 and type U130 in the Reference box to jump to cell U130.

Okay, you have seen what you are facing. You can put it down slowly, ma'am, and step away from the spreadsheet. Close it. (And if you are prompted about saving the changes, close it without saving.)

Creating a Query in Power Query to Clean Up Accounting Data

In Power Query terms, a *query* is a series of steps you create to pull data into Power Query and perform a number of actions on the data. In the background, Power Query records those steps (using a language called M, which has nothing to do with the M of James Bond, although it is pretty powerful). A query is somewhat similar to a macro in that you record steps and can later play them back. Once you've recorded a query in Power Query, all you need to do to perform the steps again is change the data source you apply the query to.

Instead of doing all the clean-up the old-fashioned way, you can use Power Query to clean it up and make it pivot table ready (with headings, no blank rows, no blank columns, no extra total rows,...).

1. Open a new file in Excel.

2. Select Power Query | From File | From Excel (see Figure 6-1).

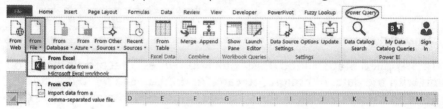

Figure 6-1

3. Navigate to where you have stored 06_Accounts_data_dump_01 and click it. Click OK. Note that this file has already been converted to a table.

4. In the Navigator window that appears, click the Accounts sheet on the left and then click the Load button (see Figure 6-2). You are nearly there.

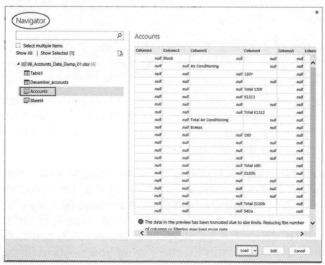

Figure 6-2

5. Click Query | Edit Query (see Figure 6-3). In the Power Query window that appears, on the right is the Applied Steps window, which lists the steps you take to clean up the data (see Figure 6-4).

Figure 6-3

Figure 6-4

The Applied Steps window essentially provides a record of what you do with the data. Although you can't "undo," you can remove a step by clicking the x to the left of the step (see Figure 6-5). However, if you click on the x next to steps that are taken toward the beginning of a query, you may sometimes receive a warning.

Figure 6-5

> **Note** Once you have your data in Power Query, it's important to remember that most of the operations you need are on the Home tab.

In Figure 6-5, you can see that some of the columns already have names because this data has been converted to a table. You can also see that some of the cells contain the word *null*. Power Query inserts *null* wherever there was a blank cell in the original data.

You need to remove all the columns that contain nothing but *null*. You can click the filter at the top of a column to see what is in the column. When you do this, you find that the following columns have no data (i.e., contain nulls only): Column 1, Column 5, Column 6, Column 7, Column 8, Column 9, Column 10, Column 11, Column 12, Column 13, and Column 14. The following steps walk you through what you need to do to clean up your data:

1. Remove each column that contains nothing but nulls—Column 1, Column 5, Column 6, Column 7, Column 8, Column 9, Column 10, Column 11, Column 12, Column 13, and Column 14—by highlighting it, right–clicking, and selecting Remove (see Figure 6-6). Or if you hold down the Ctrl key, you can highlight more than one column at a time and then right-click and select Remove. Keep in mind that you are removing these columns because you do not want any blank columns in the final data set.

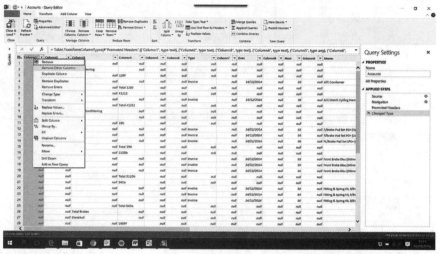

Figure 6-6

> **Survival Tip** Make sure you keep your mouse pointer near the column heading when highlighting the columns that contain only nulls. If you don't, many of your right-click options (e.g., Rename) will not appear.

2. Remove the last column, Balance, the same way you've removed the other columns.

> **Note** Remember that if you accidentally delete something you didn't want to delete, you can remove the step by clicking on the x next to it in the Applied Steps window (refer to Figure 6-5).

3. Right-click column 2, select Rename (see Figure 6-7), and type the name `Category`. (Figure 6-7 shows the column already renamed Category.)

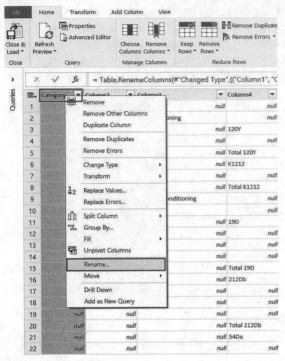

Figure 6-7

4. To fill down the Category column, select Transform | Fill | Down (see Figure 6-8).

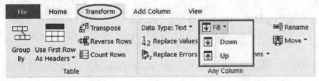

Figure 6-8

5. Right-click column 3, select Rename, and change the name to Subcategory.

6. To fill down the third column, click Subcategory and select Transform | Fill | Down.

7. To fill down the Type column, click Type and select Transform | Fill | Down.

8. To filter the Type column to exclude nulls, click the Type heading. Click the filter triangle and make sure Null is not ticked (see Figure 6-9).

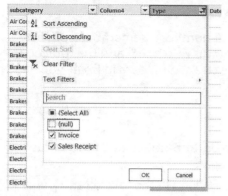

Figure 6-9

9. Filter the Date column to exclude nulls. Again, do this by clicking the Date heading, clicking the filter triangle, and removing the tick beside Null.

10. Because column 4 now contains just null values, remove it.

11. The data is looking good now, so type the name 06_Accounts_ clean_up in the Name row of the Query Settings pane (just above the Applied Steps window).

12. Select Home | Close & Load | Close & Load (see Figure 6-10).

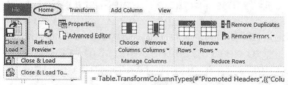

Figure 6-10

Excel brings the data back in, and it now looks as shown in Figure 6-11.

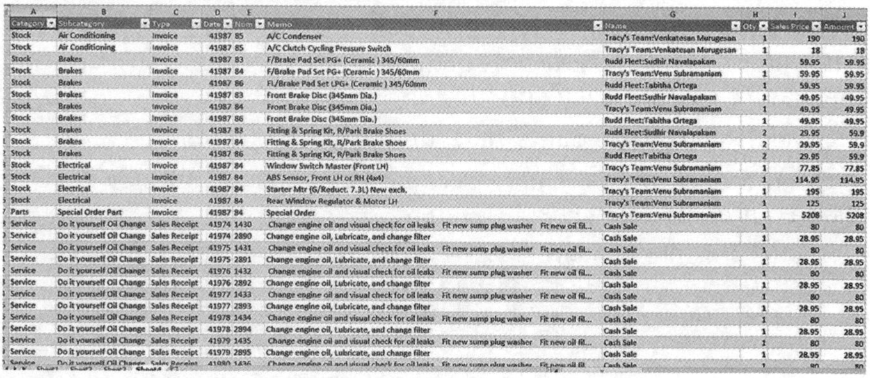

Figure 6-11

Checking Your Results in Excel

At this point, you need to check your numbers. Remember from earlier in the chapter that the total amount was 65,010.65, and the total quantity was 128. Now that you have the cleaned up data in Excel, you need to check that the data is accurate.

1. Highlight the Amount column by clicking in the top cell and pressing Ctrl+Shift+Down Arrow.

2. Check the sum calculation on the bottom-right side of the status bar. Yep, there it is: 65010.65 for the amount.

3. Highlight the Quantity column by clicking in the top cell and pressing Ctrl+Shift+Down Arrow.

4. Check the sum calculation (not the count) on the bottom-right side of the status bar. It's 128—just the number you were hoping for.

5. Now you have completely tidied up the data, and it's ready to be pivoted, so save the file as My_06_query_accounts_clean_up.

Okay, this particular data set looks great. But what about next month, when you have to clean up a new data set?

Do It Again! Do It Again!

When my son was young and I'd toss him up in the air (just a little bit…), he'd beg me "Mom, do it again," and that's what we are going to do here (the repetition, not the tossing up in the air). Now you need to clean up a different file, but you need to clean up all the same stuff in it that you just cleaned up in 06_Accounts_cata_dump_01. Pretend that the file you're cleaning up here is the next month's file.

1. Open the file 06_Accounts_data_dump_02. (Note that the data here has already been converted to a table.)

2. Check the quantity in cell Q109: It's 146. Also check the amount in cell U109: It's 57,751.82. Make a note of these figures because you'll be using them as a cross-check later on.

3. Close the file 06_Accounts_data_dump_02.

4. Open the file My_06_query_accounts_clean_up. (You may have to click a button that says Enable Content

> **Note** This file contains the Power Query code (called M) that was created in the background when you cleaned up the file 06_Accounts_data_dump_01. You are now going to use this code to clean up the 06_Accounts_data_dump_02 file.

5. Select Power Query | Launch Editor (see Figure 6-12).

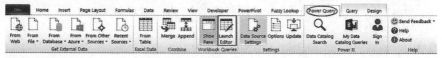

Figure 6-12

6. Find Source in the Applied Steps window and click the cog to the right of it (see Figure 6-13).

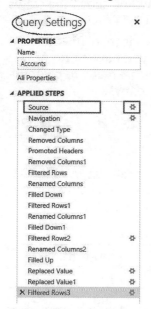

Figure 6-13

7. In the dialog box that appears, click the Browse button (see Figure 6-14), navigate to 06_Accounts_data_dump_02, and click OK.

Excel

Browse for or type a file URL.

File Path

C:\Users\Anne\OneDrive\PivotTableBook\Working Files\06_Power_Query\([Browse...]

Open File As

Excel Workbook

[OK] [Cancel]

Figure 6-14

> **Note** The path that appears for your file will not be what you see here because you will have the files stored in a different location.

8. Select Home | Close & Load | Close & Load (refer to Figure 6-10). You are now back in Excel again.

9. To check your sum, highlight the Amount column by clicking in the top cell and pressing Ctrl+Shift+Down Arrow. You see in the status bar that the sum is 57751.82.

10. To check your quantity, highlight the Quantity column by clicking in the top cell and pressing Ctrl+Shift+Down Arrow. You see in the status bar that the sum is 146.

Holy moly! That was FAST! That's right: You've cleaned up the next month's file, and it took less than a minute! All you have to do now is save this file under an appropriate name, and you are ready to pivot the data. (Honestly, every time I do this, I'm impressed myself.)

Converting Unpivoted Data to a Pivoted Format

Excel works best with data that is presented vertically, as in Table 6-1. This is also called normalized data, as you've heard a time or two in this book.

Table 6-1: Unpivoted Data in Correct Normalized Format

Date	Invoice Number	Product	Amount
1/11/2015	00123	Apples	100
1/11/2015	00123	Oranges	500
1/11/2015	00123	Pineapples	150

But Table 6-2 shows how most Excel users assemble their data.

Table 6-2: Already Pivoted Data

	1/11/2015	1/11/2015	1/11/2015
Apples	100		
Oranges		500	
Pineapples			150

The problem is that as more invoices and products are added, Table 6-2 becomes more and more unwieldy, and extracting data out of it becomes harder and harder. On the other hand, even though it seems counterintuitive, Table 6-1 is tailor made for use with a pivot table. And it also allows you to more easily add new invoices and products. The idea is for data to be vertical rather than horizontal.

There are quite a few ways in Excel to "unpivot" data, but usually they involve a few formulaic gymnastics. You'll be glad to know that the steps for unpivoting data in Power Query are relatively straightforward.

If you open the file 06_Data_for_unpivot, you see that it is classic pivoted data (but has already been converted into a table). However, if you want to do a pivot table on it in order to do more analysis, you couldn't do it as is. Here you are going to use Power Query to unpivot this data. You are also going to pull this data into Power Query in a slightly different way than you did earlier in the chapter.

1. With the file 06_Data_for_unpivot open, select Power Query | From Table and note that Power Query automatically selects and pulls in all the data in it (see Figure 6-15).

Figure 6-15

2. Highlight column 1 (Row Labels) and select Transform | Unpivot Columns | Unpivot Other Columns (see Figure 6-16).

Figure 6-16

> **Note** In step 2 you are unpivoting the columns, but you could also do it by highlighting all columns *except* column 1 and then selecting Transform | Unpivot Columns | Unpivot Columns.

3. Right-click column 1, select Rename, and change the name to Account Name.

4. Right-click the Attribute column, select Rename, and change the name to Month.

5. To convert the month entries to date format, highlight the column Month. Then check the Home tab, and you can see that the dropdown says Text. Now click on the triangle beside this and choose Date. Note that the months now become dates. You need the data in this format if you want to use months as a way to summarize the data.

6. For Value, to make sure the numbers are numbers, highlight the column and check the dropdown on the Home tab to ensure that it says Decimal Number, as shown in Figure 6-17. You don't need to rename it.

Figure 6-17

7. Type the name `Accounts` in the Name row of the Query Settings pane (just above the Applied Steps window), as shown in Figure 6-18.

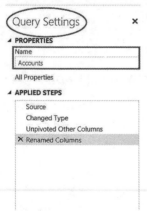

Figure 6-18

8. Select Home | Close & Load | Close & Load.

9. Excel brings back the data, and it's ready to be converted to a pivot table.

Note In this example, you have pulled the data straight into Power Query from a table. Because you have done it this way, there is no "cog" available (like the one shown in Figure 6-13). This shows that you can just do a Power Query "on the fly." If you did want to re-use the query, you would have to ensure that the data is in a separate file and then pull it in as discussed earlier in this chapter. You can practise creating an on-the-fly query by using the file 06_Data_unpivot_02 (which has a similar format to 06_Data_for_unpivot but contains just 6 months of data.)

Creating a Query in Power Query to Merge Data Sets

You've already learned how to use Power Query to clean up an accounting data dump and also how to use Power Query to convert unpivoted data to a pivoted format. Now you're going to see how to use Power Query to merge data sets. For this scenario, you will be working with three separate files for three separate months.

In the folder 06_Merge_folder there are three files that you need to combine:

- 06_Merge_files_January
- 06_Merge_files_February
- 06_Merge_files_March

Note that these files are all in CSV format. If they were Excel files, you would need to take a different approach than is described here.

Note These files use the European date structure dd/mm/yyyy.

You need to combine these files into a single file, but before you do, you need to do a quick check of the starting totals:

- When you open up 06_Merge_files_January and highlight the total, you get the following: count = 639, total = 3993599
- When you open up 06_Merge_files_February and highlight the total, you get the following: count = 639, total = 3995819
- When you open up 06_Merge_files_March and highlight the total, you get the following: count = 639, total = 4007314

So for all three files, you get the following: total count = 1917, summed total = 11996732.

1. Close all three of the files you want to combine and select Power Query | From File | From Folder (see Figure 6-19).

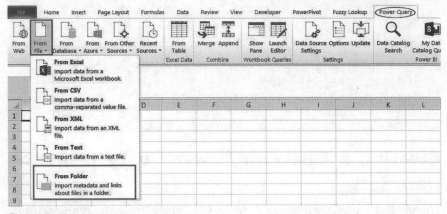

Figure 6-19

2. In the Folder dialog box that appears, click Browse (see Figure 6-20) and navigate to the folder where you have stored the file and click OK. You are now in Power Query, and one of the columns has the title Extension.

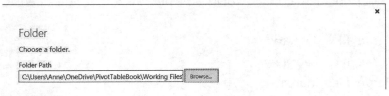

Figure 6-20

3. If you have any other type of files in the folder, filter in the Extension column so you see just the CSV files (see Figure 6-21).

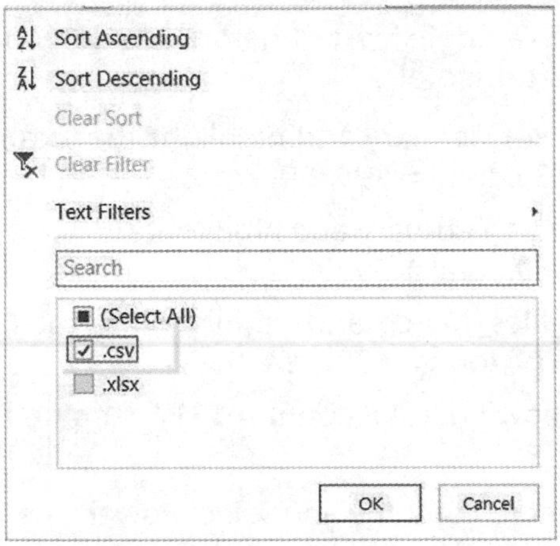

Figure 6-21

4. Click the double arrow beside the Content column (see Figure 6-22). This automatically combines the files together and you will see the content of the three of them listed.

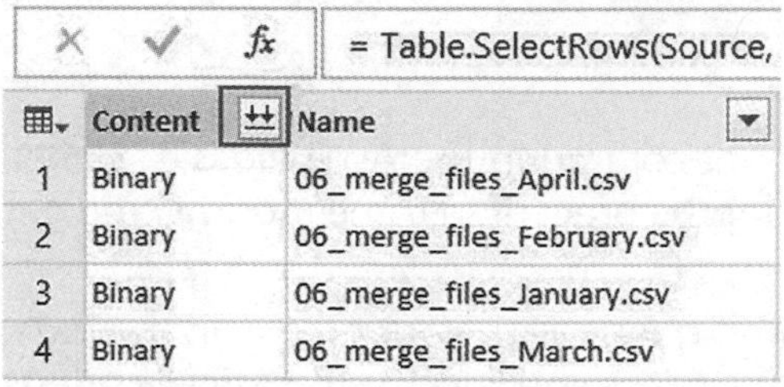

X	✓	fx		= Table.SelectRows(Source,

⊞▾	Content	↔	Name	▾
1	Binary		06_merge_files_April.csv	
2	Binary		06_merge_files_February.csv	
3	Binary		06_merge_files_January.csv	
4	Binary		06_merge_files_March.csv	

Figure 6-22

> **Note** If *any* of your chosen files are not in proper CSV format, the query will not work at all. The file should have been saved as CSV (comma delimited), with the extension.csv. If this is not the case, you need to save it in this format.

5. Because in each file the Line Item entry has no data attached to it, remove the entry from each file (by highlighting the Line Item column and filtering to remove it, making sure everything *except* Line Item is ticked in the Line Item column).

6. For the Amount column, highlight the Amount column and on the Home tab, ensure that the dropdown is set to Decimal Number (to ensure that any numbers with decimal places are picked up).

7. Select Home | Close & Load | Close & Load. The file comes back into Excel, where you can check your numbers.

8. To check your sum, highlight the entire Amount column by clicking in the top cell and pressing Ctrl+Shift+Down Arrow. You see in the status bar that the count is 1917. To check your quantity, highlight the Quantity column by clicking in the top cell and pressing Ctrl+Shift+Down Arrow. You see in the status bar that the sum is 11996732. These numbers match the ones you got when you added together the numbers in the original three files.

9. Save this file as Quarter_1_power_query.

Running Your Query to Merge Data Sets

Your data-merging query is great so far, but what happens next month, when you get another month's worth of data to add? You should be able to guess by now that Power Query makes it a piece of cake.

1. Open the folder 06_Merge_folder. Add to it the file called 06_Merge_files_April from the folder 06_Power_Query. This folder should now contain four files:

- 06_Merge_files_January
- 06_Merge_files_February
- 06_Merge_files_March
- 06_Merge_files_April

Note that the total for the Amount column in the April file is 4185595. When that is added to the total for the preceding three months, you get a total of 16182327.

2. Open the file Quarter_1_power_query. With your mouse in the data, select Data | Refresh All (see Figure 6-23), and Excel automatically brings in the April numbers.

Figure 6-23

3. Highlight the totals in the refreshed file, and you get 16182327—just what you calculated it should be.

> **Survival Tip** When I was coming to grips with Power Query, I found two courses absolutely invaluable. The first one was the course offered by Ken Puls and Miguel Escobar at www.powerquery.training. The second was Mynda Treacy's www.myonlinetraininghub.com/excel-power-query-course. I highly recommend both of them.

Summary

I've covered data clean-up in two chapters of this book because in your Excel journey, you will be spending a lot of time doing clean-up. But Power Query is a game changer. Learning how to use it can be one of the most valuable time investments you can make. You can't really control how people enter data. Dirty data is a fact of Excel life. But using Power Query is like having a dishwasher instead of doing dishes manually.

Chapter 7 Beyond the Pivot Table: Power Pivot

Pivot tables and Vlookup()s are like bread and butter for many Excel users. But they can be temperamental and fraught with infuriating idiosyncrasies. And before you can use them, you are probably going to spend a lot of time just cleaning up data. Learning to use Power Query is going to give you a distinct advantage. But even when you're a Power Query master, if you're like a lot of other Excel users, you're facing larger and larger data sets—which usually means setting up a pivot table and then going for a cup of tea as Excel laboriously grinds through the calculations.

To address the unique problems of working with loads of data, Microsoft has brought out a free add-in called Power Pivot. It is designed to work specifically with huge data sets and to eliminate the need for Vlookup()s. This chapter provides only a brief introduction to this amazing new add-in. You'll learn enough here to get going with Power Pivot, but be sure to check out the resources suggested at the end of this chapter for more information.

Essentially, Power Pivot allows you to combine multiple different data sources (e.g., Excel files, Access files, CSV files)—without Vlookup()s— and then create a pivot table from that data. The beauty of Power Pivot is that when you need to run the report again, you just refresh the data connection and the pivot table, and you are done.

Also, Power Pivot can handle huge amounts of data very easily because of the compression technology behind it. (However, I still recommend that you use a 64-bit processor, and of course extra RAM never hurts.)

Installing and Locating Power Pivot

You can download Power Pivot for free from the Microsoft site and install it using the instructions provided there. Note that before you download the product, you need to determine whether your computer is a 32-bit or 64-bit machine. You also need to check if it's available for your version of Office. Your vendor should be able to tell you. If you are working in a corporate environment, you probably need to ask your IT department to install Power Pivot for you.

When the installation is complete, you should see a new PowerPivot tab on the ribbon (see Figure 7-1).

Figure 7-1

Somewhat like a skittish racehorse, Power Pivot can sometimes disappear. Usually the following steps help you retrieve it:

1. In Excel, select File | Options.

2. In the Excel Options dialog that appears, select the Add-ins tab from the bottom-left side (see Figure 7-2).

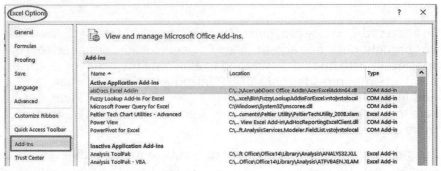

Figure 7-2

3. Scroll through the Add-ins list until you locate Power Pivot. (Note that if it has disappeared from the ribbon, it might be in the Inactive Applications list.)

4. At the bottom of the dialog, choose COM Add-ins from the Manage dropdown (see Figure 7-3) and click OK.

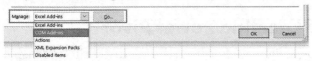

Figure 7-3

5. In the COM Add-Ins box that appears, make sure the Power Pivot for Excel box is ticked (see Figure 7-4) and click OK. The Power Pivot ribbon tab should now appear. However, if it still hasn't appeared, you may need to restart Excel to get it to show up.

Figure 7-4

Note The following site provides a list of known Power Pivot installation issues: http://mrx.cl/1SrIW0v

Before You Start Using Power Pivot

There are a few things you need to know before you start using Power Pivot:

You need to create a date table. (You can see an example of this in the 07_Powerpivot folder. It is the file called 07_Date_table.)

While you do not need to use Vlookup()s, certain rules still apply. For example, the tables have to be linked via some sort of relationship.

Before you create a pivot table through Power Pivot, it will look as though you have no data in your Excel sheet (unless you are using an Excel table within the file).

It's a good idea to store all the files you need in one folder.

To learn how to use Power Pivot in this chapter, you are going to work with a very typical monthly task: You need to prepare a set of accounts that includes the totals for the current month and the year-to-date figures.

Note Assume that your chart of accounts is up to date. This is just a listing of all the account numbers and descriptions you use to prepare your accounts. If you work as an accountant, part of your real-life work will probably include checking that there are no new account codes. You do that via Vlookup()s to identify the infamous #N/A errors when, for example, you're comparing last month's chart of accounts to this month's chart of accounts to identify any new accounts. For more information, see Chapter 4, "The Vlookup() Function: An Excel Essential."

All the files used in this chapter are in the folder 07_Powerpivot:

- The file 07_Chart_of_accounts is the nominal ledger code listing—that is, a list of all the codes allocated to various transactions, such as sales, expenses, etc. (Note that in this chart of accounts, there are no balance sheet listings.)

- The file 07_Transactions lists all the transactions and should include at least a nominal ledger code (Account, in this case), a date (Transaction_date), and an actual amount (Actual).

- The file 07_Date_table is an Excel sheet that lists all the dates in the data and has columns indicating what week/month/quarter the data relates to. It should have one column (ideally called Date) that contains just a list of unique dates. The data in these files spans three years, from July 2011 to June 2013, and these are the dates in this file. (The file uses the European dd/mm/yyyy entry format.) Note that this data has been formatted as a table and includes the month name and month number. You are going to mark this as a date table after you import it into Excel.

In this chapter, all the files are Excel files, though it is possible to combine and pull in other types of data.

Getting Your Data into Power Pivot

1. Open Excel. You see a file that will look blank until you pull in the pivot table from Power Pivot later.

2. Select PowerPivot | PowerPivot Window (see Figure 7-5).

Figure 7-5

3. In the Table Import Wizard that appears, click on Other Sources and scroll down until you get to Excel File option down at the end (see Figure 7-6). Click it and then click Next. Next you will pull in the three files, one by one. They are going to appear as three separate tabs in the Power Pivot window, and you have to do each one separately.

Figure 7-6

4. In the next step of the wizard, click Browse and navigate to where you have stored the 07_Powerpivot folder. (Note that if you already have the file open, you will be prompted to close it.) Select the 07_Transactions_ listing file, give it the friendly Excel connection name Transactions, and tick the box Use First Row as Column Headers (see Figure 7-7). Click Next.

Table Import Wizard   ?   ✕

Connect to a Microsoft Excel File
    Enter the information required to connect to the Microsoft Excel file.

Friendly connection name: Transactions

Excel File Path: C:\Users\Anne\OneDrive\PivotTableBook\Working Files\07_Powerpivot\07_   Browse...

☑ Use first row as column headers.

                                    Advanced...   Test Connection

Figure 7-7

> **Note** You can filter the data even at this point by using the Preview and Filter option.

5. In the next step of the wizard, click the Transactions sheet and then click Finish.

6. Give Power Pivot a moment or two, and when the import is finished, you see a big green Success marker on the dialog box. Click Close. You now have a sheet tab called Transactions in your Power Pivot window (see Figure 7-8).

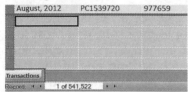

| August, 2012 | PC1539720 | 977659 |

Transactions
Record: ◄ ◄ 1 of 541,522 ► ►

Figure 7-8

> **Note** Having the sheet tabs clearly named makes importing much easier.

7. Repeat steps 4–6 for the other two files: 07_Chart_of_accounts and 07_Date_table. Use the connection name Accounts for the 07_Chart_of_accounts file. (You will be importing the Accounts sheet of this file into Power Pivot.) Use the Connection name Date Table for the 07_Date_table file. When you are finished, you should have three tabs (sheets) at the bottom, each with the name of the connection: Transactions, Accounts, and Date Table.

8. Mark your table as a date table by clicking anywhere in the Date Table tab and then selecting Design | Mark as Date Table (see Figure 7-9). (Earlier I mentioned converting 07_Date_table to a date table. You want to do this because you will be using a Power Pivot feature called Time Intelligence later on, and having a date table clearly marked as such will give you fewer problems.)

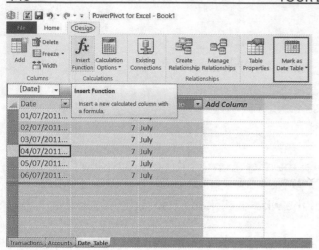

Figure 7-9

Linking the Data Sets Together

Familiarity with Access and databases will give you an advantage at this point. In order to extract data from multiple data sets, you must first link them together. As with Vlookup() (and, indeed, all matching/lookup functions), you must have something matching, and one of the data sets involved has to contain unique values of that matching set. For example, in your three tabs in the Transactions table, the account number will be repeated many times. However, in your chart of accounts, any individual account number will be entered only once. In the same way, in your date table, the entries in the Date column are unique (every date has been entered only once), but there will be many repeating dates in the Transaction_date column in the Transactions table. So the next step is to link up the tables.

Table 7-1 shows the matching fields in this instance.

Table 7-1: Matching Fields

Tab	Field (Many)	Linked To	Name of Field
Transactions	Transaction_Date	Date_Table	Date
Transactions	Account	Accounts	Account

This is how you do it:

1. Click the Transactions tab.

2. Click on any of the Transaction_date entries and then select Design | Create Relationships. You should see a Create Relationship dialog, as shown in Figure 7-10. Note that Transaction_date appears automatically in the column for the Transactions table.

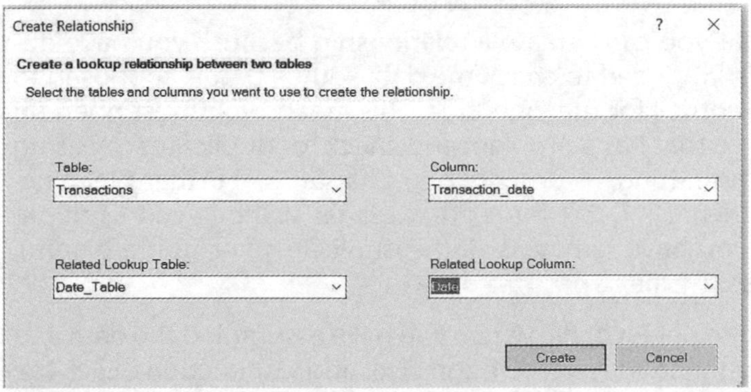

Figure 7-10

3. In the Create Relationship dialog, click the Related Lookup Table dropdown and choose Date_Table. From the corresponding Related Lookup Column dropdown, choose Date. Click Create. You have created a relationship between these two tables.

4. To create a relationship between the Accounts table and the Transactions table, start by clicking the Transactions tab, click any of the Account entries, and then select Design | Create Relationships.

5. In the Create Relationship dialog that appears, click the Related Lookup Table dropdown and choose Accounts. From the corresponding Related Lookup Column dropdown, choose Account. Click Create. You have now created a relationship among these three tables.

> **Note** If the two fields have the same name, Power Pivot automatically selects that name for you in the Related Lookup Column field.

> **Survival Tips** When you create relationships as in this section, it is best to start from the "many" side. For example, in this example, the account number would be repeated many times in the Transactions table but appears *once* in the Accounts table.
>
> If you find that you can't create a relationship because you have duplicate values, you need to check the data source that is supposed to have unique entries for the "one" side. This means you must open up the data source that has a problem and check for duplicates (by using conditional formatting, as described in Chapter 3, "Further Cleaning, Slicing, and Dicing"). Don't forget that blanks will be seen as duplicates. When you have removed all the duplicates (including blanks), save and close the file.
>
> Return to the Power Pivot file where you have assembled the data and refresh the connection: Select Design | Existing Connections, click the connection you want to update, and then click Refresh. Power Pivot brings in the new tidied up data, and you should be able to create the relationship.

Creating a Pivot Table from the Combined Data

When you have put all your data together and created the links, the next step is to create a pivot table from the data.

1. In Power Pivot, select Home | PivotTable | PivotTable (see Figure 7-11).

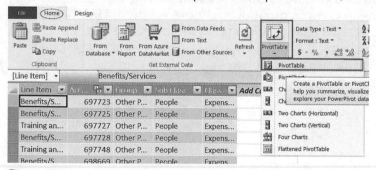

Figure 7-11

2. When Power Pivot suggests a new worksheet, click OK. Power Pivot puts the pivot table into Excel. If you check your usual PivotTable Field List, you now see that all three tables are represented.

Next, you will construct two pivot tables from this data:

- Profit and Loss by Month
- Profit and Loss Year to Date

Creating the Profit and Loss by Month Pivot Table

To begin creating the Profit and Loss by Month pivot table, you start by dragging down the fields into the PivotTable Field List as follows:

1. Into the Row Labels area, from the Accounts table, drag down Class and Sub Class (see Figure 7-12).

2. (If Net Revenue appears below Expenses, just click the Net Revenue heading and drag it up to the top.) In the pivot table, filter out Head-count by clicking Row Labels and unchecking Headcount Statistics in the dropdown list (see Figure 7-13).

Figure 7-12

Figure 7-13

3. Drag Month-name from Date_Table down into the Column Labels area (see Figure 7-14).

Figure 7-14

At this point, you may have realized two things: First, you need to have a way of identifying the years; second, the months are organized alphabetically instead of chronologically (see Figure 7-15). So you need to go back into Power Pivot to make some changes and then refresh the data.

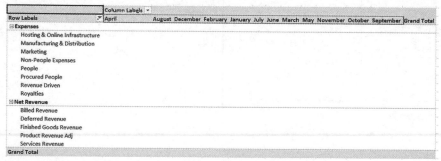

Figure 7-15

To identify the years, follow these steps:

1. Select Power Pivot | PowerPivot Window (see Figure 7-16). Excel takes you back to the Power Pivot window.

Figure 7-16

2. Click in the Date_Table sheet.

3. Click in the blank column beside Fiscal Date and enter the following formula:

```
=year(Date_Table[Date])
```

Note that the column now renames itself Calculated Column 1.

4. Right-click the top of Calculated Column 1, choose Rename Column, and type `Year`.

5. To refresh the pivot table to show the new data, click the Switch to Workbook icon (see Figure 7-17). When the PowerPivot Field List warns that the data has been modified, click Refresh (see Figure 7-18). Year now appears as a field in the Date table.

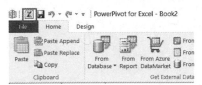

Figure 7-17

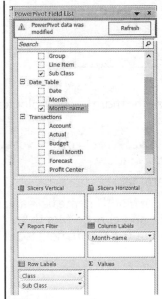

Figure 7-18

6. Drag Year (from the Date_Table) onto Slicers Vertical (see Figure 7-19) and then resize this newly created slicer.

Figure 7-19

To organize the months chronologically instead of alphabetically, follow these steps:

1. Select Power Pivot | PowerPivot Window. Excel takes you back to the Power Pivot window.

2. Click Date_Table.

3. Click in the Month-name field and select Home | Sort by Column | Sort by Column and choose Month to sort the Month-name field into the same order as the Month field (see Figure 7-20). Click OK.

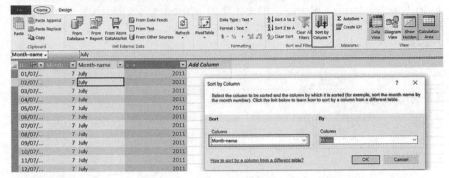

Figure 7-20

4. To refresh the pivot table to show the new data, click the Switch to Workbook icon. When the PowerPivot Field List warns that the data has been modified, click Refresh. The months are now in chronological order.

You still have to get a calculation, and to do that, you are going to create your first measure.

Creating a Measure

Usually to create a pivot table, you just drag down your numbers (e.g., Actual from Transactions), but in this case you are going to create a number of measures. A *measure* in Power Pivot is a formula that you can use in the Values part of a PivotTable Field List instead of dragging down a field (as you did when you created a pivot table in Chapter 5).

The beauty of using measures is that once you have created one, you can reuse it in all your pivot tables.

Follow these steps to create your first Power Pivot measure, called Actual-Total:

1. Click in the pivot table you just created.

2. Click on the Transactions table in the PowerPivot Field List on the right side.

3. Select Power Pivot | New Measure (see Figure 7-21).

Figure 7-21

4. In the Measure Settings dialog that appears, set both the Measure Name and Custom Name text boxes to `Actual-Total` (see Figure 7-22).

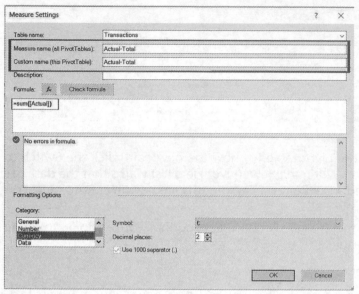

Figure 7-22

5. Click in the Formula box (beside the =) and type `sum([` to bring up a list of the fields in the Transactions table.

6. Double-click Actual. Your formula should now read `=sum([Actual])`.

7. Click Check Formula, and you get the message No errors in formula.

8. Convert your measure to currency by selecting Currency from the dropdown at the bottom of the Measure Settings dialog.

9. Now you need to add one further tweak to this formula. In accounting systems, revenue appears as a negative number, but usually that's not what you want to see in your accounts. So to get around this, edit the measure in the Measure Settings dialog box to read as follows:

```
=Sum([Actual])*-1
```

> **Note** If you have already closed the Measure dialog box, you can edit the measure by clicking on it in the Values part of the PowerPivot Field List and then clicking on Edit Measure (see Figure 7-23).

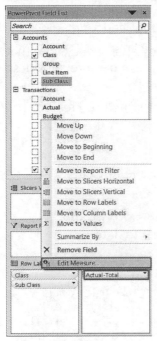

Figure 7-23

This has the effect of making the revenue look like positive numbers and the expenses look like negatives, which is how you expect to see your numbers in a profit-and-loss account.

10. Click OK.

This measure now appears in the pivot table as Actual-Total, and you have completed the Profit and Loss by Month pivot table. You can view the profit and loss for each year by choosing a year from the slicer.

Creating the Profit and Loss Year to Date Pivot Table

To create the Profit and Loss Year to Date pivot table, you repeat the same steps you took to create the Profit and Loss by Month pivot, but in this case you use a different measure, which you can call YTD (Year to Date).

1. Select Power Pivot | PowerPivot Window. Excel takes you back to the Power Pivot window.

2. In Power Pivot, click Home | Pivot Table | Pivot Table. When Power Pivot suggests a new worksheet, click OK. Then drag down the fields into the PivotTable Field List as follows:

- Into the Row Labels area, drag down Class and Sub-class. (If Net

Revenue appears below Expenses, just click the Net Revenue heading and drag it up to the top.) Filter out Headcount.

- Drag Month Name down into the Column Labels area. (Note that Power Pivot remembers how the months have been re-sorted, so you don't have to re-sort the months again.)

At this point you have your basic Power Pivot structure created. The next step is to create the measure for this.

Creating the YTD (Year to Date) Measure

1. Click in the pivot table and then click the Transactions tab.

2. Select Power Pivot | New Measure.

3. In the Measure Settings dialog that appears, set both the Measure Name and Custom Name text boxes to `YTD` (year to date).

4. Click in the Formula box (beside the =) and type `=totalytd([` to bring up a list of fields and measures (marked with `m`).

> **Note** In this instance, you are going to use one of Power Pivot's time intelligence functions, called TotalYTD, along with the Actual-Total measure you have already created. The TotalYTD function requires two things: a measure to calculate the total (which in this case will be Actual-Total and the dates you want to use (which we have in Date_Table).

5. Double-click [Actual-Total] and type `, D` to bring up Date_Table.

6. Choose `Date_Table[Date])`. Your formula should now read `=Totalytd([Actual-Total],Date_Table[Date])`.

7. Click the Check Formula button, and you get the message No errors in formula.

8. Convert your measure to currency by selecting Currency from the dropdown at the bottom of the Measure Settings dialog.

9. Click OK.

Presto! Your YTD numbers are done. You can double-check them by dragging your Actual-Total measure down under Values in your Power-Pivot Field List.

You can put Actual-Total above YTD (Year to Date) as shown in Figure 7-24.

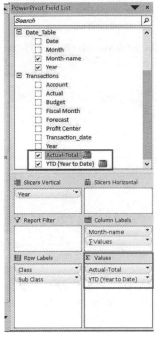

Figure 7-24

Choose 2012 from the slicer (Year) and then when you check your numbers, you can see that the grand total for January Actual-Total is -147,523,083.87, and the grand total for February Actual-Total is -117,824,079.37 (Figure 7-25), and if you add those two together (to give you the February Year to Date), that's -265,347,163.24, which is the same as the grand total for the February YTD (Year to Date). Alas, this company is *not* in good shape.

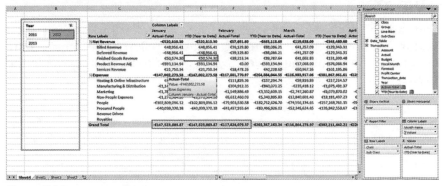

Figure 7-25

Note In Ireland we use euros (€), so some of the figures use this currency symbol

You can select Home | Refresh | Refresh when your data changes to refresh and bring in new numbers (see Figure 7-26).

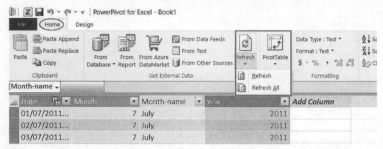

Figure 7-26

Recommended Resources

At this writing, the main player in the Power Pivot field is Rob Collie (www.powerpivotpro.com), who writes in a witty, accessible manner about the joys of Power Pivot. He has a great online course:

www.powerpivotpro.com/self-paced-online-video-training/

In terms of online training resources, I again really recommend the following:

• Mynda Treacy's www.myonlinetraininghub.com/power-pivot-course

• Chandoo's excellent course
  http://chandoo.org/wp/resources/power-pivot-videos/#3

Summary

Power Pivot is where Excel is going. You can get ahead of the pack if you start dipping your toes into it now. Data analysis is becoming more and more important, and Power Pivot is going to be a big player in the future.

Appendix Data Validation Techniques

Creating data validation dropdown lists will by itself make your Excel life much much easier. However, you can exercise even more control on data, and this appendix describes some other data validation techniques.

Restricting Number Sizes

Let's say you want to ensure that people can only enter values between certain numbers. Follow these steps:

1. Highlight the entire column or click in the top cell and press Ctrl+-Shift+Down Arrow to select the area you will be applying data validation to.

2. Select Data | Data Validation.

3. On the Settings tab of the Data Validation dialog that appears, make the following changes (see Figure A-1):

- Choose Whole Number.

- Choose Between from the Data dropdown.

- Enter 10 for Minimum and 20 for Maximum.

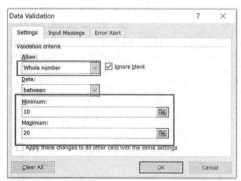

Figure A-1

4. Select the Input Message tab and in the Input Message field, enter a message that will appear when someone clicks the cell (e.g., `Please enter a number between 10 and 20`). See Figure A-2.

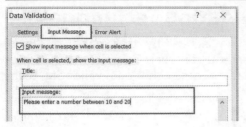

Figure A-2

5. Select the Error Alert tab and in the Error Message field, enter an error message that will appear when someone doesn't obey this rule (see Figure A-3).

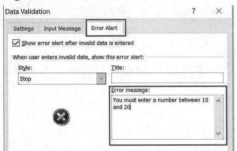

Figure A-3

6. Click OK. Now when you look at the area where you have applied the data validation, you see a popup message, as shown in Figure A-4. Also, if a user tries to enter a value that is not between 10 and 20, he or she sees the message shown in Figure A-5.

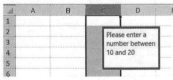

Figure A-4

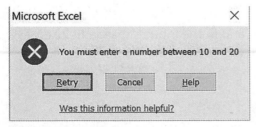

Figure A-5

Restricting Date Entries

Now let's say you want to make sure that people can only enter appropriate dates. The process is much the same as the process described in the preceding section. Follow these steps:

1. Highlight the entire column or click in the top cell and press Ctrl+-Shift+Down Arrow to select the area you want to apply data validation to.

2. Select Data | Data Validation.

3. In the Settings tab of the Data Validation dialog that appears, choose Date and in the Data dropdown, choose any of the following that are appropriate (see Figure A-6):

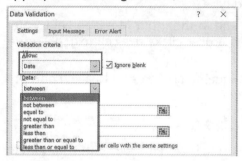

Figure A-6

- **Between:** Enter the start date and end date. Any date between these two will be accepted.

- **Not Between:** Enter the start date and end date. Any date *not* between these will be accepted.

- **Equal to:** Enter the date here. Only this date will be accepted.

- **Not Equal To:** Enter the date here. Any date *except* this date will be accepted.

- **Greater Than:** Enter the date of the day before the first acceptable date. Only dates *after* this date will be accepted.

- **Less Than:** Enter the date of the day after the last acceptable date. Only dates *before* this date will be accepted.

- **Greater Than or Equal To:** Enter the date of the first acceptable date. Only dates *on* or *after* this date will be accepted.

- **Less Than or Equal To:** Enter the date of the last acceptable date. Only dates *before* or *on* this date will be accepted.

For example, you could type `=today()` in the Date box and select Less Than to restrict date entry to only dates in the past.

Restricting Text Length

Say that you want users to be able to enter only an eight-digit number (e.g., a staff ID). This is how you do it:

1. Highlight the entire column or click in the top cell and press Ctrl+-Shift+Down Arrow to select the area you want to apply data validation to.

2. Select Data | Data Validation.

3. In the Settings tab of the Data Validation dialog that appears, choose Text Length, choose Equal To, and type 8.

4. Select the Input Message tab and in the Input Message field, enter a message that will appear when a user clicks the cell (e.g., `Please only enter 8 characters`).

5. In the Data tab dialog, choose Equal To and enter 8 to allow only entries that are eight characters long.

Extending Data Validation

What if the data validation you're using is working well, but you want to extend it? Try this:

1. Highlight cells that already contain the desired data validation as well as areas to which you want to extend the data validation.

2. Select Data | Data Validation.

3. Click Yes when you get the message that says "The selection contains some cells without Data Validation settings. Do you want to extend Data Validation to these cells?"

4. In the Data Validation dialog box that appears, click OK.

Applying Data Validation to Another Part of a Sheet

If you want to apply your data validation to another part of the same worksheet, follow these steps:

1. Click on cells that contain the data validation you want and select Home | Copy.

2. Highlight the cells to which you want to copy the validation and select Home | Paste.

3. In the Paste Special dialog that appears, select Validation (see Figure A-7).

Figure A-7

4. Click OK. Excel copies the validation to the cells you highlighted.

Identifying Duplicate Entries in a List

The easiest way to identify duplicate entries is to use conditional formatting, like this:

1. Highlight your data by clicking the top cell and pressing Ctrl+-Shift+Down Arrow.

2. Select Home | Conditional Formatting | Highlight Cells Rules | Duplicate Value.

3. In the Duplicates dialog that appears, click OK. Excel applies red conditional formatting to all entries that have been entered two or more times.

Simple Normalization (Getting Crossways Data to Go Lengthwise or Vice Versa)

This is a great little gem. Let's say you have data in this format:

Mon
Tue
Wed
Thu
Fri
Sat
Sun

but you actually need it in this format:

Mon	Tue	Wed	Thu	Fri	Sat	Sun

What to do? Simple:

1. Highlight the data and click Home | Copy.

2. Click where you want the data to go choose Home | Paste | Paste Special.

3. In the Paste Special dialog that appears, tick Transpose (see Figure A-8).

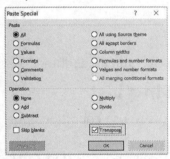

Figure A-8

4. Click OK.

Presto! The work is done. Don't you love it when a plan comes together!

> **Survival Tip** There are times when this method does not do what you want, and it takes a little Excel magic to massage your data into the format required. For example, an odd quirk I discovered as I was writing this book is that you can't use the method just described with table data. You have to convert it to a range first by clicking the table and selecting Design | Convert to Range.

Unpivoting Data

Excel guru John Walkenbach devised an elegant unpivoting technique that Mike Alexander (another Excel guru) describes at his website:

http://mrx.cl/1MNLykl

Allen Wyatt, another Excel guru, also created a rather elegant unpivoting technique:

http://excelribbon.tips.net/T012614_Transposing_and_Linking.html

I really recommend signing up for his Excel Tips, which are always useful.

Index